*The Man
Who Mapped
Consciousness*

HAY HOUSE TITLES
OF RELATED INTEREST

YOU CAN HEAL YOUR LIFE, the movie,
starring Louise Hay & Friends
(available as an online streaming video)
www.hayhouse.co.uk/louise-movie

THE SHIFT, the movie,
starring Dr. Wayne W. Dyer
(available as an online streaming video)
www.hayhouse.co.uk/the-shift-movie

***

THE LETTING GO GUIDED JOURNAL:
How to Remove Your Inner Blocks to Happiness, Love, and Success,
by Dr David R. Hawkins, MD, PhD

BEYOND ILLUSION:
Exploring Perception, Ego, and Meditation on the Path to Truth,
by Dr David R. Hawkins, MD, PhD

THE MAP OF CONSCIOUSNESS EXPLAINED:
A Proven Energy Scale to Actualize Your Ultimate Potential,
by Dr David R. Hawkins, MD, PhD

All of the above are available at your local bookstore,
or may be ordered by visiting:

Hay House UK: www.hayhouse.co.uk
Hay House USA: www.hayhouse.com®
Hay House Australia: www.hayhouse.com.au
Hay House India: www.hayhouse.co.in

The Man Who Mapped Consciousness

THE AUTHORIZED BIOGRAPHY

The Life and Legacy of
DR DAVID R. HAWKINS

Susan Hawkins

HAY HOUSE

Carlsbad, California • New York City
London • Sydney • New Delhi

Published in the United Kingdom by:
Hay House UK Ltd, 1st Floor, Crawford Corner,
91–93 Baker Street, London W1U 6QQ
Tel: +44 (0)20 3927 7290; www.hayhouse.co.uk

Text © David and Susan Hawkins Revocable Trust, 2025

Cover design: Barbara LeVan Fisher
Interior design: Julie Davison

The moral rights of the authors have been asserted.

All rights reserved. No part of this book may be reproduced by any mechanical, photographic or electronic process, or in the form of a phonographic recording; nor may it be stored in a retrieval system, transmitted or otherwise be copied for public or private use, other than for 'fair use' as brief quotations embodied in articles and reviews, without prior written permission of the publisher.

The information given in this book should not be treated as a substitute for professional medical advice; always consult a medical practitioner. Any use of information in this book is at the reader's discretion and risk. Neither the authors nor the publisher can be held responsible for any loss, claim or damage arising out of the use, or misuse, of the suggestions made, the failure to take medical advice or for any material on third-party websites.

A catalogue record for this book is available from the British Library.

Tradepaper ISBN: 978-1-83782-333-8
E-book ISBN: 978-1-4019-7958-4
Audiobook ISBN: 978-1-4019-7980-5

10 9 8 7 6 5 4 3 2 1

This product uses responsibly sourced papers, including recycled materials and materials from other controlled sources. For more information, see www.hayhouse.co.uk

The authorized representative in the EU for product safety and compliance is Penguin Random House Ireland, Morrison Chambers, 32 Nassau Street, Dublin D02 YH68, Ireland. https://eu-contact.penguin.ie

Printed and bound by CPI Group (UK) Ltd, Croydon CR0 4YY

*"Straight and narrow is the path. . . .
Waste no time."*
Gloria in Excelsis Deo!

CONTENTS

Introduction	1

PART ONE: The Infinite Presence, 1927–1946

Chapter 1: Early Life: A Journey into Curiosity	9
Chapter 2: Shaping Resilience and Discipline	27

PART TWO: All That Is, 1946–1979

Chapter 3: Education and Influences	39
Chapter 4: The Career-Focused Man	49
Chapter 5: The Cost of Addiction	59

PART THREE: The High Pass, 1979–1999

Chapter 6: Another Turning Point	71
Chapter 7: A World of Human Potential	85
Chapter 8: Westward and Inward	107
Chapter 9: Charting the Map of Consciousness®	119
Chapter 10: The Work Begins	133

PART FOUR: The Final Doorway, 1999–2012

Chapter 11: The Work Meets the World	141
Chapter 12: The Home Stretch	157

Acknowledgments	163
The Map of Consciousness®	165
Accomplishments of Dr. David R. Hawkins	167
Summary of Books by Dr. David R. Hawkins	195
Notes	211
References	217
About the Author	223
About Dr. David R. Hawkins	225

INTRODUCTION

"Society needs visionaries of means, not dreamers of ends. Once we have the means, the ends will reveal themselves." [1]

In the world of psychology, spirituality, and the intricate tapestry of human consciousness, there has never been anyone quite like David. As his wife, I have had the privilege of sharing many of life's most intimate moments with a man whose existence was a symphony of curiosity, discovery, and transformation. Born in 1927 and taking his leave from this earthly stage in 2012, David's life story is like a rollercoaster through the peaks and valleys of human understanding. This biography is not merely a chronicle of a remarkable life but an intimate journey sharing the profound impact he had on the world.

David, or Doc, as most people called him, was born on June 3, 1927, in Milwaukee, Wisconsin. He was the eldest of two children and grew up in an era marked by significant historical events, including the Great Depression and World War II, during which he did his part for his country, enlisting in the navy at age 17 and entering active duty in 1945. From an early age, it was clear that David possessed a curious and inquisitive mind. He was not content with merely observing the world around him; he sought to understand it in its entirety.

Growing up in the Hawkins household, young David was exposed to intellectual stimulation in a nurturing cocoon of knowledge. His father—a classical pianist with degrees in chemical and mechanical engineering—and his mother—a high-society flapper and skilled pianist and composer in her own right—fostered an environment where learning was not a chore but a joy. I came to appreciate how this early exposure to the wonders of the mind played a significant role in shaping the man he would become.

David's journey of self-discovery was not confined to his childhood. It extended into his years of formal education. He attended Milwaukee State Teachers College (now the prestigious University of Wisconsin–Madison) and later Marquette University School of Medicine (now the Medical College of Wisconsin), where he pursued and received both a B.S. and M.D. in medicine. It was during this time that he laid the foundation for a deep understanding of science, which would later enable him to navigate the intricate world of the human psyche with precision and insight.

David's interests evolved from the medical field to psychiatry and psychology. His educational journey was marked by a fervent desire to explore the depths of the human mind and to help people who were struggling with addiction and alcoholism—issues that were present in his own family history and that he, too, struggled with. He completed his psychiatric residency at Columbia University and, always with his eye on the future, was soon treating patients at his own clinic, North Nassau Mental Health Center, on Long Island. David approached patient care with an expansive, and perhaps eclectic, worldview, focusing on the person as a whole—body, mind, and spirit—not just as their symptoms. Though this is a more common view of healthcare now, David was incorporating alternative modalities to individualize care for every patient long before it was accepted and despite what other doctors and professionals were saying.

David's transition from a medical student to a renowned psychiatrist was not without its challenges. The world of psychiatry in the mid-20th century was marked by evolving paradigms and shifting ideologies. Yet David's unwavering commitment to understanding the human psyche led him to become a prominent figure in the field. It was during this phase of his life, an exploratory time of questioning and seeking, that he became dedicated to unraveling the mysteries of human consciousness and what might lie beyond. He was introduced to A Course in Miracles, the Sedona Method, rebirthing, and more, all influences that sparked his intellect and convinced him there was more to discover beyond what could merely be seen or scientifically proven in the world.

Up to this point, his accomplishments might have been enough for another person—they were certainly enough to fill a whole lifetime and possibly more. But David sensed there was more—to know, to learn, to share with others for the benefit of all.

At 52, he shed his life as a successful psychiatrist with a thriving clinic and private practice in New York City and moved to the arid desert of Sedona, Arizona. Colleagues and others in his circles thought he was crazy to give up the prestige and accolades, but things like that never mattered to David.

He entered a time in the '80s we later referred to as his "monastery of one," a time of deep contemplation, meditation, research, and synthesis of all the wisdom he'd accumulated—medical, spiritual, and metaphysical. His study of different spiritual methods and alongside teachers of different traditions in the '80s helped further his understanding of consciousness, and he began to discern the various levels of consciousness that were possible. This is when the Map of Consciousness® was born.

This was also the time when I met David, a chance—or perhaps not so chance—encounter at a country-western dance class. Upon seeing each other, we both felt an instant familiarity, a spark, a connection that linked up beyond this lifetime. About six months into our relationship, he shared the Map of Consciousness® with me, and I immediately sensed that this was something huge, urging him to share it with a wider audience. His dedication to understanding the nature of consciousness was unlike anything I'd ever experienced. He then developed the initial draft of *Power vs. Force* in 1990.

From that point onward, David's life took on a new direction, though it was really the direction his life had always been headed. He became not only a psychiatrist (having passed the Arizona psychiatric licensing exam at age 59) but also a spiritual guide. As with many spiritual teachers, his work was not fully understood or accepted by everyone. He had such a challenging time trying to find a publisher for *Power vs. Force* that we started our own publishing company, Veritas Publishing, to release it. Once it was published, the Map of Consciousness® became a guiding light for those seeking to elevate their awareness and deepen their understanding of human consciousness. That book has now been translated into 17 languages and was only the first of more than a dozen books he wrote and published in his lifetime. We flew all over the country and the world, offering lectures and classes on

Introduction

the work as well as always expanding, testing, and learning more about the work ourselves.

But what about David the man I knew intimately? Behind the accolades and academic achievements was the man I knew and loved. As his wife, I was privy to the private moments, the conversations that took place in the quiet of our home, and the experiences that shaped him as a husband, a father, and a friend.

David was not just a brilliant mind; he was a man of deep compassion and love. He had a warm and infectious sense of humor that could light up any room. He was a devoted father and a loving partner. He cared deeply for all people, always championing kindness and compassion. He also had a great love for animals all his life, and was often happiest while working in the garden, tending to the chickens, or just spending time with his beloved dog, Kelsey. I watched him as he juggled the demands of his professional life with the joys and challenges of our family life.

As his widow, I have the unique opportunity to share not just his public achievements but also the intimate moments that made up our life together. I hope to provide a glimpse into the man I knew—a man who was not only a thinker and a spiritual teacher but also a compassionate and loving human being. This is more than a biography; it's a heartfelt journey, an invitation to experience his life and witness the extraordinary legacy he left behind. I hope to show that as we delve into his thoughts, his lectures, and his personal musings to get a glimpse of the brilliance that ignited his spiritual wildfire.

From his work as a science-based psychiatrist to his teachings as a spiritual teacher, David has left behind a treasure trove of insights into the human psyche and consciousness that are as mind-blowing as they are soul-nourishing. As you follow his journey, you'll come face-to-face with the revelations that turned his world upside down and elevated the consciousness of anyone fortunate enough to encounter his work. David didn't just gift us with theories and diagrams; he handed us a road map to Truth. His visionary Map of Consciousness® isn't just a scholarly endeavor; it's an invitation to elevate our understanding of existence.

So, join me as we embark on a life that transcends the boundaries of the physical, and venture into the vast realms of the heart, the spirit, the intellect, and the very soul of consciousness itself. As David wrote in *Letting Go*, "The world can only see us as we see ourselves."[2] Are you ready to change the way you see yourself? David catalyzed that change, and now I am that change. You are that change. Together, we can transform our lives and the very fabric of humanity as we know it.

PART ONE

THE INFINITE PRESENCE
1927–1946

CHAPTER 1

EARLY LIFE: A JOURNEY INTO CURIOSITY

The early chapters of Dr. David R. Hawkins's life were written against the backdrop of historical turbulence, with the Great Depression looming large and World War II casting its long shadows. But David was destined to traverse the intricate landscapes of human consciousness. Little did he know that these formative years would shape the contours of his intellectual curiosity, laying the foundation for a life dedicated to unraveling the mysteries of the mind and spirit.

PARENTS FROM DIFFERENT WORLDS

Ramon Nelson Hawkins, David's father, was a man with a foot in practicality and a foot in curiosity—a trait that he certainly passed on to his children. He was a classical pianist who fronted an orchestra called Red Hawkins at the University of Wisconsin, but he also held degrees in chemical and mechanical engineering. He would go on to manage some of the earliest gas stations and repair shops in the 1920s and '30s, when the automobile industry was first booming.

David's mother was Alice-Mary Hawkins, née McCutcheon. Her grandfather, David G. Hooker, had been the Democratic mayor of Milwaukee from 1872 to 1873 and continued to be a prestigious lawyer after his term in public office. He became general counsel of Northwestern Mutual Life Insurance Company and lived a prosperous life, having six children from two wives.

Though Alice-Mary, born in 1907, never knew her grandfather (who passed away from heart disease in 1888), she benefited from his trust and was raised in Milwaukee's high society. Alice-Mary had a deep love of music, becoming a pianist and advocate for the arts. Coming of age in the Roaring Twenties meant that she grew up experiencing a freedom that women had long been fighting for, including the right to vote. She had a vast intellectual curiosity, exploring scientific innovation, music, psychology, art, and more throughout her early life. She was a true high-society flapper, living a dazzling blend of glamour, liberation, and social rebellion. With her daring fashion choices, lively demeanor, and insatiable thirst for adventure, Alice-Mary embraced the newfound freedoms of the era with her fellow flappers by boldly challenging traditional norms and redefining womanhood in the modern age.

For the flapper in Milwaukee, evenings were a whirlwind of excitement and extravagance, centered around the city's bustling social scene. Lavish parties, soirées, and speakeasies provided the perfect backdrop for these vivacious women to showcase their flair for fashion and their boundless joie de vivre. Dressed in the latest trends of the time—knee-length dresses adorned with fringe, feathers, and beads, paired with stylish cloche hats and strands of pearls—flappers were the epitome of chic sophistication.

Ramon and Alice-Mary met in the mid-1920s and had an instant connection through their passion for music. They were quite the pair with Ramon's dashing reddish hair and Alice-Mary's striking green eyes and petite build. Dancing the Charleston and the foxtrot with abandon, they embraced the exhilarating rhythms of jazz music, which served as the soundtrack to their glamorous escapades. Though they came from vastly different circles of society—Ramon was a working-class man and Alice-Mary a social elite—their love could not be stopped, and they eloped on April 29, 1926, a minor scandal briefly surrounding the marriage.

About a year later, on the evening of June 3, 1927, the curious soul that the pair named David Ramon Hawkins came into this world. He was soon followed by a sister, named Sally-Claire, who was born in 1929, the same year that the stock market crashed, leading to the beginning of the Great Depression.

Sally-Claire, vivacious and outspoken almost from birth, was David's polar opposite. He preferred his own company and was an earnest, thoughtful child. His sister, on the other hand, had no qualms initiating conversation with strangers or causing a bit of a ruckus, much to David's chagrin. The Hawkins children were taught not to use curse words, but Sally-Claire would invent her own, and, with a glint in her eye, she would use them until even David was laughing along with her. He envied her straightforward bravery and extroverted nature and would often channel her vivacity later in life when he had to do talks in front of large crowds.

THE EARLY HAWKINS HOUSEHOLD

In the quiet neighborhoods of the Milwaukee suburbs, the Hawkins household was a sanctuary for intellectual curiosity and the pursuit of knowledge. Young David entered a world where learning was not just encouraged but celebrated as an essential part of the fabric of daily life. The suburbs at this time were highly rural, and David grew up learning to care for chickens, ducks, goats, rabbits, and dogs as well as a large garden in the summers.

David always had a strong bond with animals; he simply understood them and seemed to speak their energetic language. During this time, he had a pet duck named Peep Peep that he would carry around with him while he worked around their little farm. When he saw a spider, he would lift Peep Peep up to get the spider—the duck loved these tasty snacks! Peep Peep was a loyal and smart duck who was very attached to David, always running to greet him whenever David would come outside.

David learned to care for animals from his father. Ramon would tell his children a story about how he once went hunting as a boy—something that was expected of all boys where he grew up. Upon encountering a deer, he lifted the 30-gauge rifle. But then, as David recalls, his father

> looked in the deer's eyes, and in that instant, he couldn't kill it. He saw what it was. He saw the consciousness shining out of the deer. The deer loves its life and is aware of its existence the same as you, no different at all. It just doesn't call itself "deer." But he saw that it was really existence itself coming forth as awareness of existence and he couldn't kill it. So, he never killed anything. I've never killed anything,

Early Life: A Journey into Curiosity

either. This is because you're aware that it loves its life. All that exists loves its life to the same degree that you love your life.[1]

Duck and chicken eggs, goat milk, rabbit meat, all kinds of fresh produce, and well-trained puppies provided a source of extra income for the cash-strapped family, and from an early age, David harbored an entrepreneurial spirit. He would take on whatever jobs were available, including becoming the neighborhood babysitter and setting pins at the local bowling alley.

When there wasn't a job available, David would create one, such as collecting scrap metal to sell. David and his father would also go to the dump and find things that people had thrown away. They looked for items that were broken but potentially fixable. With a little ingenuity and elbow grease, they would fix up electrical appliances or furniture and then sell the revamped items. They would then go to the store to buy treats or things they needed. This taught David about the value of his own hard work as well as a lot of skills in maintenance, construction, and even mechanical engineering. One time, David found a small airplane glider that he loved, and after fixing it up, he played with that glider for hours, watching it defy gravity and sail across the yard.

The family also valued their time together and looked forward to spending time with each other. Every week, whether in snow or sun, the whole family would take a drive in their Model A car—David and Sally-Claire in the rumble seat—to go to a nearby neighbor and pick up two loaves of bread. This was a weekly extravagance that the whole family enjoyed, often eating a whole loaf of the just-out-of-the-oven bread on the car ride home!

The young Hawkins children were also immersed in the humanities, visiting museums as well as going to see ballets and symphonies whenever possible. Along with their love of music, both Ramon and Alice-Mary were voracious readers, a trait that they instilled in both their children. David especially remembered his mother's avidity for the written word, which became a cornerstone of his early exposure to literature. Through her, David discovered the profound impact of words, an impact that would later manifest in his own eloquent writings and teachings.

The family could be seen weekly at the library, loading up an eclectic assortment of books. David stuck to nonfiction and quickly mastered the ability to speed-read, only needing to glance at each page to consume its contents. The gentle rustle of pages turning and the scent of well-loved books filled the Hawkins home, creating an atmosphere where intellectual exploration was not only encouraged but cherished. During a time when most people—the Hawkinses included—were struggling financially, David learned that books could be an escape as well as a way to become rich in ideas, even if he couldn't be rich in money.

In this fertile environment, young David's imagination took flight. His early years were marked by a blend of academic pursuits and a voracious appetite for knowledge beyond the classroom. He was drawn to books, not merely as repositories of facts but as gateways to uncharted territories of thought. The library became his sanctuary, a place where he could satiate his intellectual curiosity and feed his burgeoning imagination. In this microcosm of intellectual diversity, the inquisitive mind of a budding polymath found ample nourishment.

Early Life: A Journey into Curiosity

The Hawkins household was, in essence, a harmonious fusion of scientific inquiry and humanistic exploration. Ramon and Alice-Mary, each with their unique perspectives and backgrounds, created an environment where the boundaries between the scientific and the artistic blurred. The dichotomy between the rational and the creative was not seen as a division but as a synthesis—a coming together of seemingly disparate elements that enriched the intellectual landscape of young David.

The dinner table, rather than being a mere setting for family meals, became a forum for discussions that delved into the mysteries of biology, philosophy, and the human condition. These conversations became a catalyst for David's insatiable curiosity about the world. Both parents encouraged exploration and questioning, though Ramon could also be strict in his conservative viewpoints.

His parents didn't just talk the talk, they also walked the walk, as this curious anecdote relates. In the summer of 1939, a severe reaction to poison ivy landed 12-year-old David in the hospital. The onset of septicemia from the allergic reaction posed a serious threat to his well-being. As doctors grappled with the complexities of treating the worsening condition, Alice-Mary turned to an unconventional source for a solution. She sought the expertise of a medicine woman at the Wisconsin Dells Indian Reservation. Armed with traditional knowledge, the woman applied an Indigenous remedy to David's ailment. The salve worked like a miracle, curing the severe poison ivy reaction that had baffled medical professionals.

Alice-Mary's quick thinking and openness to all forms of knowledge saved her son that day, and she also instilled in him the idea that true answers don't necessarily come from institutions in power. She herself suffered from several chronic conditions and had learned that the doctor's remedies didn't always do the trick. This incident, while a personal testament to David's resilience and the efficacy of alternative healing methods, also served as a harbinger of the themes that would later thread through his work. The convergence of traditional wisdom, spirituality, and the healing of mind and body became a narrative that resonated not just in the corridors of the Wisconsin hospital but in the expansive landscape of David's evolving consciousness.

In interviews and reflections, David later recalled how his parents recognized and nurtured his affinity for learning. From a young age, it was evident that David's intellectual journey would be marked by a continuous quest for understanding and a passion for uncovering the mysteries that lay beyond the surface.

NURTURING THE SEEDS OF CURIOSITY

Both sets of David's grandparents lived near enough that they also had a profound impact on his early life. His McCutcheon grandparents, Frank and Ashley-Alice, also valued literature and owned an expansive library that David was free to borrow from. They were also close friends with William Atwood, the head of the science department at Milwaukee State Teachers College (which later became Wisconsin State). Atwood had a flourishing collection of plants, insect specimens, and reptiles—all surely fascinating to a young boy. By Atwood's side, David learned entomology, pinning and studying thousands of species. David and Sally-Claire also often spent the weekend with their Hawkins grandparents, Frank and Mary Jane, who exposed them to opera, Shakespeare, and religion.

Early Life: A Journey into Curiosity

As a child, David exhibited a prodigious intellect. Every adult in David's life encouraged his spirit of inquiry, prompting him to explore beyond the confines of traditional education. His inquisitive mind was apparent in the questions he posed about the world around him, hinting at a thirst for knowledge that would later become a defining characteristic of his life. He was the kind of child who didn't have to put much effort into getting good grades, often bored in school and with most ordinary childhood activities. Most of his true knowledge was self-taught. David was interested in philosophers like Plato, Aristotle, Plotinus, and Socrates since childhood, considering them to be his "mental companions."[2]

He also wore thick glasses and was small-statured, all of which made him a target for bullies. Though he briefly tried sports like football and swimming to fit in, he wasn't suited to them. "As a kid," David later said in one of his lectures, "I was always getting beat up. So, my grandfather took me to Richie Mitchell's gym and said, 'Teach him how to fight.' I was never interested in fighting and all these gruesome wrestling crap that kids did. I mean, lots of kids were disgusting when I was a kid."[3] David was even smaller than the smallest weight class the gym had available—flyweight—and so they created a new one, called mosquito weight.

At the gym, David learned to leverage his small size and speed to his advantage. "The first fight after that, I won. I was so fast that he didn't know what hit him and I always hit him in the nose—*wham*, like that!—and then I was out before he could hit me. He'd get a bloody nose—end of fight. I thought that was pretty good," David said of the time.[4] After bloodying the nose of a vicious school bully, he was mostly left alone.

As a testament to his early exposure to a rich tapestry of influences, David found himself drawn to artistic expression.

He tried many things and succeeded at almost everything he tried. For example, when he tried his hand at watercolors in grade school, he won an award. David also learned to play the piano and the violin. With his quick mind, he easily memorized music, eventually writing his own music with guidance from his mother, who was a bit of a composer herself. Later, despite his natural talents, he decided not to pursue art or music as a career for practical, financial reasons.

It was in this atmosphere that David's early inclinations toward exploration and understanding began to flourish. The dichotomy of influences between science and the humanities set the stage for his later multidisciplinary approach—a distinctive feature that would distinguish his contributions to fields as diverse as psychiatry, consciousness studies, and spirituality.

FIRST ENCOUNTERS WITH HIGHER CONSCIOUSNESS

David's parents were Episcopalians, and Ramon was especially strict about religion. The family attended services at three churches: Cathedral Church of All Saints, St. Paul's Episcopal, and Christ Church.

All Saints was their main church of worship, where they could be seen for major religious observances and most weekends. It was farther away, though, so for convenience, the smaller, local Christ Church made do when the family couldn't drive into Milwaukee. David became an active participant in the St. Paul's church choir, along with being an acolyte to the bishop. His melodious voice soon led him to become a soloist in the 8th or 9th grade—an accomplishment that hinted at the multifaceted nature of his talents. Ramon accompanied the choir on the organ. The ethereal

Early Life: A Journey into Curiosity

resonance of hymns, coupled with the reverberations of the organ, became a symphony that echoed not just through the church but through the corridors of David's consciousness.

David initially accepted religion without much question, first appreciating the sublime beauty that could be found in church, especially at All Saints, which was an ornate, Gothic cathedral. The strictness with which his parents practiced their religion made him extremely committed to the purity of his soul, almost to the level of obsession. He was always worried about sinning between confession on Saturday afternoon and communion on Sunday morning—a time when his soul was supposed to remain clean. He feared that any unclean or angry thought might make God take revenge in the form of some disaster, such as a car crash or being struck by lightning.

Because of this fear, David would always try to wait as long as possible, going to the very last time slot for confession at four o'clock. That way, there would be as little chance as possible of sinning before communion the next day. As David later remembered:

> You lived in fear that this spot on your soul would appear. You keep your eyes focused on the ground, keeping careful control of your thoughts and your mind that you won't have a sinful thought. You can make it probably from five on Saturday to seven o'clock on Sunday morning without a sin. And just as you're on your way to church with the top down on the '29 Model A Ford, you pass a forty-two-by-ninety-six-foot big advertisement of Jantzen swimsuits. Here's this big, blonde lady, forty-two feet long—there goes the innocence. At age six it wouldn't bother you, but

at fourteen, it was.... Thirty-two-foot-long swimming suit. I won't ever forget that.[5]

In 1939, an event occurred that altered his thoughts on religion and the course of his life forever. At this time, 12-year-old David was tasked with the role of a paperboy, so he was always out in the dark, delivering papers to his northern Wisconsin neighbors before dawn. The winters were especially brutal, with whiteout snow and windchill far below zero. His neighbors knew how difficult this could be, and at one house there would always be a wrapped-up fried egg sandwich waiting in the mailbox for him. This thank-you gift was always warm and comforting, giving David energy to continue along his route.

One wintry night, David navigated a blizzard's relentless onslaught under the cover of darkness and realized he could go no farther. He felt he was practically freezing to death and sought refuge from the merciless 10-below-0 winds. His desperate quest led him to a 20-foot-high snowbank on the side of the highway that blocked the merciless winds. David scooped out a hole in the side of the snowbank with his numb hands and curled up inside, hoping to wait out the storm.

Within this icy sanctuary, an exceptional transformation unfolded. As the biting cold drove him inward, an exquisite state of consciousness manifested. Amid the frozen confines, the boundaries of thought dissolved, and his mind fell into a profound silence. "Within a few seconds," David says, "I began to experience a state of relaxation, and a state of profound warmth began to come over the body. It was a state of exquisite pleasure, and I began to forget about the body. The body just did not seem to exist anymore, and instead, an incredible blissful state of peace came over me."[6] A Presence,

Early Life: A Journey into Curiosity

timeless yet powerfully gentle, pervaded the surroundings. Its overwhelming Love eclipsed the usual workings of David's thinking mind.

In this moment, time seemed to be suspended. The awareness of unity with eternity superseded rational thought, and any notion of a personal self faded away. "The 'I-ness' of the Presence revealed itself as Allness"—a cosmic force beyond the confines of all universes.[7] Descriptions failed to capture its essence; it was unspeakable, invisible, all-encompassing, and inexplicable, eluding the constraints of language and naming.

A metamorphosis followed. The perennial fear of death, an ever-present specter in the human experience, dissipated like morning mist in the warmth of sunlight. Life, liberated from the shackles of fear, continued its course spontaneously, guided by its innate rhythm. This Infinite Presence, as David later called it, "is always present, and its realization occurs of itself when the obstacles to that realization are removed. It is therefore not necessary to study the truth but only to let go of that which is fallacious."[8]

In a later lecture, David recalled the moment:

> There was no desire to breathe or re-enter the body or become one with the body again. There was no interest in the body. I mean, the state is complete and total. There's no need for a body, desire for a body; there's no physicality that has any appeal. My father had discovered where I was. He traced the paper route. We had a '29 Model A Ford—it is hysterical—a '29 Model A Ford for which we had paid fifteen dollars, by the way. And, Dad found me; so here is this shaking of my knee, and I'm asked to do that which I did not want to do more than anything. But if I had

not resumed breathing and come back to it—come back to the body, he would have thought I was dead. He believed in the body—you know, if the body is dead, you're dead. So, I could see he believed that I would be dead, which would cause great grieving, and I loved my father a great deal, so I breathed.[9]

David did not have words to explain what he'd experienced to his father—what he later learned was a kind of near-death experience. In the hushed sanctuary of that snowbank, he'd undergone a transcendent journey. After, he wrestled with the implications of it on the religion that he'd so revered. He was no longer afraid of death and had experienced something that "went beyond bliss and became an eternal, infinite state, far beyond ordinary consciousness."[10] He found he could no longer be so fearful of the potential outcome of small sins. It simply didn't matter anymore. This profound state was his first taste of what was beyond the confines of the ordinary, and it became a closely guarded secret, an experience he shared with no one until many years later.

A few years later, 15-year-old David was walking in the woods when he experienced another moment of realization. "I was a devout, in fact, a scrupulous Christian," David later recalled in a lecture. "I was a boy soprano, and I still adore church and great cathedrals. So one day I'm walking through the woods, and all of a sudden, the totality of man's suffering was revealed. The totality of the suffering of all mankind throughout all of time. . . ."[11]

David also wrote about this pivotal moment in his book *Discovery of the Presence of God*. "There came unasked a massive revelation of the totality of human suffering throughout all time which resulted in an overwhelming feeling of shock and dismay that 'God could allow such conditions to occur.'"[12]

"In that instant I became an atheist," David said. "I hated any god that could allow the sheer dimension, as well as qualities of what I saw. I became a *rabid* atheist."[13] But this led to another pressing question: "If there was no God, then what was the core of the truth of existence?"[14]

This question would push David to seek answers for the next 30 years. "But I was integrously atheist," David said. "The atheist can be integrous if it is not an intellectual position of pridefulness and vanity and ego. But if one's commitment to truth is profound and you are a religionist, there's going to be a moment when you're going to go through a violent convulsion because a lot of what one holds dear is going to run smack up against commitment to absolute truth. And that's what happened with me."[15]

After this experience, David stopped going to church, which caused many disagreements with his father, who simply couldn't square his son's newly acquired atheism. But David wouldn't be swayed; from his freethinking point of view, truth could only be discovered through actual experience, not through the blind faith of religious dogma.

THE END OF CHILDHOOD

That moment was the beginning of David's coming-of-age, and by the time he was 16, he had broken off what he'd considered the shackles of his childhood and early beliefs. During the second two years of high school, he was not interested in the general education curriculum, and his grades suffered. His teachers noted that he was exceptionally intelligent, but they couldn't persuade him to apply himself to his studies.

He became a bit of a troublemaker along with Louis Rove and Manfred Waller, friends whom he called Louie and Manny. Fellow atheists and outcasts themselves, the three built a friendship based on their mutual admiration of philosophy and their love for adventurous fun. David and his buddies loved listening to operas and reading about great philosophers. They were always in the midst of some ongoing debate or conversation about the arts, philosophy, and other topics that most kids their age had no interest in at all.

This is also the time when David began smoking and drinking alcohol. Both of David's parents would have been considered alcoholics, but that word wasn't in wide use at the time—everyone drank. For Ramon and Alice-Mary, though, the drinking was often to excess. David witnessed this as a child, thinking it was relatively normal. He took his first drink due to peer pressure—though he did have some curiosity and a desire to understand the effects of alcohol for himself as well. During the summer of his 16th year, he worked at a canning factory in Janesville, Wisconsin, canning, crating, and storing peas in a hot and humid warehouse. The work was strenuous, and the hours were long; often the crews would work 12 or even 16 hours each day. David recalls a particularly difficult day toward the beginning of his time in the factory when he was so tired he couldn't go on:

> Out in 110 degrees in a pea cannery, in this warehouse with no windows, I could not lift one more box. Not one more. I was never a heavyweight to begin with. Anyway, after twelve or fourteen hours in this heat and no water and god-knows-what-all, I said, "I can't do it." And then something came up, and there was this incredible decision to go through the barrier. I

crashed through the barrier and all of a sudden, the boxes became weightless. I lifted them like feathers. I could have kept going for days. And I've done that many times when I am lifting stone and all.[16]

Discovering that barrier, and—more importantly—what lay beyond it, was a moment that would push David to break barriers in other areas of his life and ways of thinking as well.

His co-workers would blow off steam by drinking, and David joined them in an effort to fit in. After that first drink, David took a liking to alcohol, especially hard liquor. The moment the bottle touched his lips, he would be filled with a warmth and easiness that he didn't often find in his daily life. The noise would stop, and he could focus on his senses. He especially loved to drink out in nature at night; his body would come alive. Unfortunately, this was the beginning of a prolonged battle for David. There was a history of alcoholism in his family, and drinking would continue to plague David for much of his life.

This brief excursion into Dr. Hawkins's early life offers snapshots of who he was, each a brushstroke in a vibrant tapestry woven with the threads of familial support, musical exploration, academic pursuits, and unexpected encounters. These glimpses are crucial to understanding who David would become, a multifaceted individual who would go on to leave an indelible mark on the realms of psychology, spirituality, and consciousness research.

CHAPTER 2

SHAPING RESILIENCE AND DISCIPLINE

As David grew older, his family faced an upheaval with the onset of World War II. Like many of his generation, he found himself drawn into the tumult of global conflict. The Hawkinses were a patriotic family with a history of military service going back several generations. David finished high school a semester early and, in December of 1944, enlisted in the United States Navy. Though he was only 17—the draft age at the time was 18—he was able to join with his parents' permission.

RECRUITMENT AND BOOT CAMP

At first, it seemed that his dream of serving his country wouldn't come true: he was 4 pounds below the required weight of 100 pounds. But after a month and a half of eating lots of protein, sugar, and bananas, he just scraped by and was on his way to basic training. His military service, although a departure from the intellectual pursuits of his earlier years, became a crucible that would forge qualities of resilience and discipline—attributes that would serve him well in the subsequent chapters of his life.

David entered the naval boot camp Recruit Training Command in Great Lakes, Illinois, with a mix of excitement and trepidation. As a recruit of smaller stature, David's journey was uniquely etched with obstacles and victories.

The physical conditioning routines were demanding, including early morning runs around Lake Michigan every day that David would try to avoid by hiding in his locker. The recruits were also put through marching drills, calisthenics, firearms training, swimming lessons, and obstacle courses that, for David, demanded not just strength but an extra measure of determination to keep pace with larger recruits. Physical strength was clearly an asset at boot camp—not just to contend with the required workouts, but also to fit in with the rest of the boys. David faced this added challenge of proving himself in an environment where physical strength often took center stage, but his strong force of determination carried him through.

Graduation day was a personal triumph for David. Standing among his fellow recruits, he had overcome physical challenges, proving that size was no obstacle to discipline and determination. Following his completion of Recruit Training Command, David transitioned to the Naval Training School in Dearborn, Michigan, beginning a specialized phase designed to enhance his skills for the imminent responsibilities ahead.

In Dearborn, David engaged in advanced seamanship training, immersing himself in the intricacies of navigation, ship handling, and maritime protocol. This curriculum extended to the operation of specialized naval equipment, where he learned the technical intricacies crucial for naval operations and communications training, with a focus on naval signaling and the use of semaphore flags. He also joined the Navy's Blue Jacket Choir, though his soprano days were far behind him.

As part of the V-12 Navy College Training Program, Dearborn provided specialized assignments tailored to individual skills and the needs of the navy. Physical fitness remained a constant, with ongoing conditioning to ensure peak physical readiness. The difficult program also provided college undergraduate credits, and it was just what David needed to stimulate and challenge his mind as well as his body. David's focus was to become a radar technician—an increasingly critical role in naval operations. His training involved mastering the intricacies of radar systems, understanding their technical components, and becoming proficient in their operation. This additional expertise positioned David as a valuable asset, contributing to the navy's growing reliance on radar technology for navigation, surveillance, and targeting.

THE PACIFIC THEATER

But the war was raging on, and all too soon, more men were needed in the Pacific theater. This was the precipice David had been working toward, the threshold of active service. Eager to do his part, the 18-year-old David did not finish his radar training, opting to ship out in late January of 1945.

His duty was aboard *YMS-46*, a Yard Class Minesweeper that had been in service since 1942. These ships, integral to naval operations during World War II, were meticulously crafted vessels designed for the perilous task of minesweeping, or clearing active mines from the water so that the navy's ships wouldn't hit them and get destroyed. The *YMS-46* was a wooden vessel similar in size and maneuverability to a yacht, and it housed 18 sailors. It had minimal armament aboard, with only three deck guns and two depth-charge projectors. But its main purpose wasn't defense, it was offense; the ship would scout the sea ahead of the armored battleships and cruisers, looking for sea mines. In their small crew, they made fierce friendships that lasted for the rest of their lives.

As a minesweeper, David encountered the challenges of dealing with different mine types, each presenting unique dangers and requiring specialized techniques for detection and neutralization. These mines included contact mines, which detonate upon physical contact with a ship's hull; moored mines, which were anchored to the sea floor; magnetic mines, which were attracted to the metal hulls; influence mines, which respond to changes in pressure or sound; and oscillator mines, which use acoustic or pressure sensors. David played a vital role in countering these threats.

He was perfectly suited to working in such dangerous conditions, as his previous spiritual experiences left him with no fear of death. David later wrote about this time that "it was as though death had lost its authenticity."[1] He faced active mines in the water with only a calm matter-of-factness, which made him a great asset when the deadly spheres came perilously close to the ship at times.

He and a colleague would stand watch for four hours at night, each wearing a gun belt with a loaded 45, ready to shoot anything that moved. Once, they were faced with a mine right up against their boat. "What happens if it goes off?" David's crewmate asked him, clearly terrified of the armed device in such close proximity.

David replied, "Well, then we die."[2] While his statement was only the truth that his colleague surely already knew,

David's complete calm nature and equanimity in the face of the ultimate end put things in perspective for the other man.

"You're right," he said, and his fear went away. There was a peace in knowing that they were doing exactly what their duty was, and David was able to instill that kind of peace in many of his crewmates.

To contend with these threats, *YMS-46* featured advanced sonar systems essential for detecting the acoustic signatures of underwater mines. Magnetic sweeping gear, an innovation crucial in countering magnetic mines, was incorporated into the design, simulating the magnetic field of passing ships to neutralize potential threats. Additionally, these minesweepers were equipped with draglines and paravanes, towed devices that played a pivotal role in cutting the mooring lines of submerged mines. The vessels were also armed with depth charges and explosive cutting devices for cases where mines were deeply anchored or resistant to other sweeping methods. As both a defensive and offensive asset, the Yard Class Minesweepers played a vital role in securing safe maritime passages during this tumultuous war with quickly advancing technology.

David's service as a minesweeper demanded courage, technical skill, and an acute awareness of the various mine types. The experience of navigating through potentially mined waters, working to ensure the safety of allied vessels, reflects a different facet of his early life—one shaped by the urgency and challenges of wartime naval operations. The skills honed in these experiences contributed to the development of a disciplined and resilient mindset, qualities that would later characterize his approach to the exploration of human consciousness.

Assigned to the South Pacific, David experienced the challenges of the region, including the relentless Typhoon Louise, which, in October 1945, caused more casualties than any single battle of the war. *YMS-46* braved the tumultuous seas, facing the formidable task of maintaining stability and safety amid the typhoon's fury, which lasted for three days, caused unrelenting winds of 80 knots (92 miles per hour), and created 35-foot waves.

During the typhoon, the storm was so powerful that most of the men were seasick and couldn't help out. David and one other mate took turns with the duty of keeping the boat afloat. They would replace each other every two hours because the work was so strenuous and tiring. When David took his shifts, the winds would be so powerful that to keep the boat from capsizing, he had to brace himself by stretching out one leg against the side of the ship and, at the same time, keeping his hands on the wheel to keep the ship steady so it wouldn't sink. By the time it passed, the typhoon had sunk 12 ships and grounded 222, though *YMS-46* was spared.

During night watch duties, David found solace and diversion by listening to classical records. The soothing melodies provided a stark contrast to the high-stakes operations and turbulent weather. Amid the darkness, the music offered a respite, a brief escape into the world of symphonies and compositions, a respite that was direly needed at times. One night during his watch, he heard a *thump, thump, thump* and couldn't figure out where it was coming from. Looking over the edge of the ship, David suddenly realized that it was a dead body, floating in the water and hitting the hull. He had to push it off the side and away. These were the grim realities of cleaning up after a war.

David also demonstrated resourcefulness and ingenuity aboard the ship. While offshore, David would procure fruit like bananas and apples, and then, using empty paint cans, he fermented the fruit to make an alcohol called Blackjack. Drinking was strictly prohibited, so he had to be careful to hide his efforts. This creative endeavor added a touch of camaraderie and levity to the challenging environment. It also helped ease the tension and fear that underpinned every day—especially aboard a minesweeper—they all knew they could die almost at any moment, and that wasn't easy to come to terms with. All his crewmates drank the clandestine alcohol, and more than half of them, David included, became alcoholics during their time in service.

AT WAR'S END

At the end of the war, David and his shipmates were able to spend some time in China, specifically in Shanghai and Formosa. They sampled local cuisine, frequented bars, and collected souvenirs. David kept an elegant ebony Buddha statue from Shanghai all his life.

David's crew wasn't the only one around celebrating the end of the war, and while they were all on the same side, there could be some competition between different crews. Some nights at the bars, David's crew would set him up at the bar with a drink by himself, and other, bigger sailors would tease David with something like "Oh, you're just a little kitty sailor." Then, David's mates would come out and a fight would start, causing a phenomenon known as "tearing up the bar" due to how destructive it could be. This was even written about in *LIFE Magazine*. David remembers one confrontation:

These guys, they have got tattoos, earrings, and stuff. I mean, they were grizzly-looking guys who'd been out to sea for a while. So, this guy says, "Hey, Shorty." That was my name henceforth—"Shorty," or "Four Eyes."

"Shorty," he says, "you know how to box?"

I said, "Well, I had lessons with Richie Mitchell, who was the former middleweight champion of the world in Milwaukee."

"Wow," he said, "we'll go up in the gun tub and go a round." So, we go up like this, and one shot and I was unconscious. Ha ha ha! He hit me once. Later I found out that he was champion of the Third Fleet. He was the most fearsome boxer I've ever seen. He was ferocious and fast. God bless him. Anyway, we're still friends.[3]

David had an inimitable way about him, and people couldn't help but to like him. Despite his physical differences or his intellectual ways that set him apart from many of his crewmates, he always proved his mettle and was a valuable part of the team.

Just after the new year, though, the *YMS-46* was headed back to the States, depositing David in San Francisco. He was honorably discharged from the navy on June 29, 1946, and always remembered his service fondly, keeping up with his shipmates through calls and letters for the next half-century.

Navigating the Yard Class Minesweeper through the East China Sea, weathering the forces of Typhoon Louise, finding solace in classical music during night watches, and exploring unconventional pastimes like homemade alcohol production—all these experiences marked David's journey in the South Pacific during World War II. His resilience and adaptability were not only vital for the operational success of minesweeping missions but also reflected the human stories woven into the fabric of naval service in times of war. David always fondly recalled his fellow sailors, and would mention the connection they still shared half a decade after their service:

> Fifty years after the war is over, all of a sudden, I start hearing from them. Imagine that, fifty years and suddenly some guy calls me and says, "Are you Dave Hawkins?"

> "Yeah."

> "Are you Shorty?"

> I said, "Yeah. I'm still short." He told me who he was, and we both broke into tears. So, everybody then, we found each other and as each one would call, we would always break into tears. I would break into tears, the guy at the other end would break into tears. You see, because that love, that love there was beyond all time.

> One characteristic of love is that with your mates back in World War II—there was a love there that was incredible, and it lasted forever. Fifty years, you didn't hear from them, and it was like yesterday. You break into tears. So that commitment to love, then, is beyond time, beyond assailing. I don't care what he's done in the meantime. It's all irrelevant. It's only the reality of the reconnection with love as a state of mind.[4]

The military service was a crucible for David, a testing ground for the principles of discipline, resilience, and camaraderie. Amid the chaos of war, he gleaned insights into the human psyche—its capacity for both courage and vulnerability, its resilience in the face of adversity, and the profound impact of trauma on the individual and collective consciousness.

The war years, though challenging, provided David with a unique perspective that would later inform his work as a psychiatrist. The intersection of psychology and the human condition became palpable as he observed the effects of war on the mental and emotional well-being of individuals. This firsthand exposure to the complexities of the human mind during times of crisis would prove invaluable in his later pursuits.

As David navigated the landscape of his early life, each chapter unfolded as a lesson in curiosity, a testament to the power of familial support, and a prelude to the intellectual and spiritual odyssey that awaited him. Little did he know that the seeds sown in his youth would blossom into a profound legacy, influencing not only his personal journey but also the lives of countless individuals seeking understanding in the realms of consciousness and spirituality.

PART TWO

ALL THAT IS
1946–1979

CHAPTER 3

EDUCATION AND INFLUENCES

After his time in the navy, David made his way home to Wisconsin, grateful for his time in the service but ready for something more intellectual to light him up. David knew he wanted to go to college. His educational journey unfolded with a trajectory that hinted at the brilliance that would later characterize his professional and spiritual pursuits.

A FUTURE IN MEDICINE

In September 1946, only three months out of the navy, David enrolled at the Milwaukee State Teachers College (now part of the University of Wisconsin–Madison). This was a pivotal juncture in his life where the foundations of his intellectual framework were laid. Here, he delved into pre-medical-study subjects like physics, chemistry, and anatomy to lay the groundwork for a future in medicine. He was also glad to reconnect with his childhood mentor, William Atwood, from whom he took courses in ornithology and zoology.

The Depression was still weighing heavily on his family, so David worked all throughout college and grad school to pay for his schooling. There was no time to read novels, go to the movies, or barely even rest. He went to classes mostly in the morning so he could work as a window washer and door-to-door salesman for roofing and siding during the rest of the day. He also had a variety of different night jobs, including bartending.

Throughout college he also worked at two movie theaters, eventually becoming a junior executive at one of them. No matter what he did, David brought all of himself to his work. He never considered any job small or beneath him; he was always grateful for the opportunity. David also had a knack for understanding people's expectations and had a quiet, understanding disposition that made people instantly like and trust him.

Two years into his studies, he transferred to Marquette University to be closer to home and save money. Though it was a Jesuit school and David was still an atheist, he felt that his time there was well spent. Despite being a minority in his beliefs, the teachers were open to his questions and freethinking ways, allowing him to debate the existence of God with them.

The university years were transformative for David. His exposure to the sciences, especially the intricacies of biology and anatomy, fueled his fascination with the human body and its intricate workings. These studies provided him with a solid scientific foundation that would later prove invaluable in his exploration of psychology and consciousness. While the academic rigors of pre-medical studies initially occupied a significant portion of his time, David's intellectual appetite was not limited to the sciences. He also engaged with a diverse range of subjects, from philosophy to literature, broadening his intellectual horizons and developing a holistic approach to understanding the human experience.

At Marquette, David got back into philosophy, a subject that had captured his interest since high school, and even earlier in his grandfather's library. He also learned about psychology and the burgeoning field of psychoanalysis. Interested in the complexity of the mind, it was here that David began forming ideas about understanding human behavior and experience. While medicine was interesting, David felt that science, in its dogged pursuit of objectivity, "excluded the essentially human elements of experience other than intellections. In contrast, psychiatry and psychoanalysis dealt with the unseen domain of feelings, options, meaning, value, significance, and the very essence of life itself."[1]

During this time, David started transitioning away from his initial dream of becoming a medical doctor and decided to become a psychiatrist. As he later wrote, "Man's dilemma—now and always—has been that he misidentifies his own intellectual artifacts as reality."[2] David believed that understanding could not come from simply examining data; we first needed to ask the right questions and use the right instruments to measure data.

"As we explore the nature of man's problems, it becomes clear that there has never been a reliable experimental yardstick with which to measure and interpret man's motivations and experiences over the course of history."[3] It was during these early theology and philosophy courses that David began fomenting this idea, which would later lead to his Map of Consciousness®.

The synthesis of science, philosophy, and spirituality began to take root in his mind, laying the groundwork for the interdisciplinary approach that would later define his work. He started an accelerated course of study at Marquette

University, finishing both his B.A. and M.D. in a much shorter amount of time.

One of the reasons that David so adamantly wanted to go into medicine was all the issues that he and his family members experienced. As noted, David and his family struggled for money throughout his childhood, and Ramon had impressed upon David that he should pursue something financially stable. A good life was one where he could support his family and didn't have to worry about money. Becoming a doctor—a highly lauded and well-paid position—would help him achieve that.

These issues in his family were also physical. Alice-Mary was often depressed and also severely asthmatic. She, Sally--Claire, and David all had intense allergies, both seasonal and food-specific. Sally-Claire was extremely frail, needing many surgeries for her multiple ailments throughout her life. Ramon suffered for multiple years with septicemia, or blood poisoning by bacteria, the body's most extreme reaction to an infection that had him in the hospital multiple times. David's parents' relationship had rapidly deteriorated at this time, pushed along by excessive drinking on both Ramon and Alice-Mary's parts. To add to their marital issues, the drinking caused Ramon to suffer from cirrhosis of the liver.

These issues would continue to plague David's family.

POST-GRAD LIFE

Before going out into the real world of medicine, all students were required to take on internships to practice their skills. David got an internship at Columbia Hospital in New York City in the pediatric ward as well as the disease-control unit, where he witnessed firsthand the polio epidemic that peaked in 1952, killing 3,145 children and paralyzing 21,269 in that year alone. In 1955, Dr. Jonas Salk's inactivated polio vaccine (IPV) was found to be effective and began being distributed in the United States. Two years later, cases dropped from 58,000 per year to only 5,600.

David found out he had a strong fear of public speaking during his internship. He found his voice would simply fail if he had to get up in front of any group of people, leading to a limiting belief that he was simply a terrible public speaker. When a time came that he had no choice but to speak aloud to present a paper in front of his colleagues, he asked himself, "What's the worst possible thing that could happen? Well, you could be terribly boring,"[4] his inner self replied, and if that were the worst, David decided he could handle it. He delivered the speech in a flat monotone that was exceedingly boring—but he did it!

Soon after that, he discovered how humor could be useful for public speaking. He would begin any speech with a self-deprecatory statement that was sure to bring laughter. "It is a way of just being at one with the humanness of the audience and discovering their compassion."[5] David found that he wasn't so bad at public speaking after all—once he'd conquered his fear around it. This would prove useful later in life when he would give lots and lots of speeches to large crowds. One of David's laws of consciousness (as explored in the book *Letting Go*) would later be "What one holds in mind tends to manifest,"[6] which was perfectly exemplified by this early experience.

During this time, David met 19-year-old Sally Louise Kenney, and they were married in 1949. Their first daughter, Lynn Ashley, was born in July of 1953 and their second, Barbara Catherine, came along in February of 1955. After Barbara was born, the young family moved to New York City.

Their first years of marriage were very hand-to-mouth; even though he was almost a doctor, the internships paid little, and he was working in excess of one hundred hours per week, which included all-night shifts every other day. This left Sally frequently alone to take care of things in their public housing home and tend to the infant.

David also made extra money as a cab driver during this time. David recalled when he was working as a cab driver, he became very good at finding alternative routes through the city and was always as efficient as possible. If he was waiting to turn left, his reflexes were such that when the light turned green, he could dart out and make his turn before the oncoming traffic even started through the intersection. The faster he was, the better he got tipped and the more quickly he could get on to his next fare.

But David loved the vibrant and constant busyness of the city. As he recalled:

> I would just walk down the street and just love everybody as they came along. People just beamed. They just loved it. You could stop anybody on the street in New York and start talking about anything.
>
> "What the hell do you think about Mayor So-and-So?" Instantly they would give you a talk. It's like you had known each other for thirty years. There's no barrier there. I love the streets of the city of New York. You can stop anybody, and everybody's a character, and it's terrific. The dialect, the whole style of what it means to be a New Yorker; there's a certain implicit understanding of it. The rights and wrongs—under certain circumstances it's not really stealing: "He left

it out." Oh, well, if he left it out, that's different. It's a totally different change of context. "He left it laying there." Well, okay, he left it laying there. Even a judge wouldn't convict you, probably. It's a whole different context of ethics and morality.[7]

By July of 1954, David had completed the rigorous internship at Columbia. Right after, David secured a residency at the New York School of Psychiatry, where he planned to pursue psychiatric training, open a private practice, and learn from some of the top psychiatrists in the country.

NO PLACE LIKE NEW YORK CITY

Soon after, David's hard work started paying off. He received a fellowship at Mount Sinai, which gave him a full salary and training with the best of the best—just as he'd hoped. He also became the supervising psychiatrist for the New York State Department of Mental Hygiene. He also became a staff psychiatrist at the New York Neuro-Psychiatric Center, a facility that offered care to low-income patients.

At this time, psychiatry mainly focused on psychoanalysis and the various interpretations, including that of Sigmund Freud, Carl Jung, and Alfred Adler. Everyone had a psychoanalyst—even the psychoanalysts themselves!

Freudian psychoanalysis, which was formed on the basis that human behavior is influenced by unconscious memories, thoughts, and urges, was the track that David decided to follow. Freud offered a model of how the mind functioned along with specific techniques for helping patients through emotional issues. Crucial to his theory were the five stages of psychosexual development. Getting fixated on any one stage would cause disruptions and emotional challenges in the person's life, and his work with patients focused on accessing repressed thoughts and feelings to free themselves and find catharsis.

Sandor Rado, one of the founders of the Columbia University Psychoanalytic Clinic for Training and Research, was a Hungarian psychoanalyst who developed a Freudian-based theory that caught David's attention. Adaptational psychodynamics was based on the idea that any living organism would evaluate its surroundings and then take on adaptations, or improvements, to increase its chances for survival, acceptance, and species perpetuation. If they couldn't adapt, mental illness could occur. Though this branch of psychoanalysis has become obscure, it applied a scientific approach that appealed to David's analytical mind. People's behavior could be studied in a methodical way that was based on biology, not just an understanding of their unconscious.

In 1956, David became the analysand of Lionel Ovesey at the Columbia Clinic. Ovesey was a resident in psychiatry at Manhattan State Hospital and received his certificate in psychoanalytic medicine from the Columbia Clinic in 1948. After that, Ovesey opened a private practice, joined the faculty at Columbia, and became a clinical professor of psychiatry at the College of Physicians and Surgeons. He was considered one of the top analysts in the city, with an office on the coveted East Side.

After beginning analysis, David began experiencing increasing neuroses during this period, including panic attacks, extreme anxiousness, and claustrophobia that left him unable to even drive through a tunnel, let alone enter an elevator or other enclosed area. Through his work with Ovesey, he uncovered that he was extremely competitive with other men. All his fears about inadequacy that had been stored up since his time as a scrawny child who couldn't compete in sports and how he was never the strongest or most manly in the navy came out as this paralyzing anxiety. Once he began unpacking this complex, the neuroses died away. As he would later write, "We start with admitting the truth that 'I am the source of my fearfulness.'"[8]

Not long after beginning analysis with Ovesey, David was plagued by nightmares about lions chasing him. He couldn't shake them; night after night the lions came after him with their wild manes shaking, their paws thundering along the ground, and their ferocious teeth flashing as they growled and drooled. David finally shared this with Ovesey, wondering if he might have some insight into what this anxiety was about.

"What's my name, David?" Ovesey asked. And it was only then that David realized that Lionel was his lion!

David would be analyzed by Ovesey four days a week for the next five years.

CHAPTER 4

THE CAREER-FOCUSED MAN

The late 1950s were booming for David—and he was busy. Along with seeing his two analysts, Ovesey and Tiebout, David's own private practice was just starting up while he was also attending to his fellowship at Mount Sinai and other responsibilities.

But this wasn't enough for David. His work at the New York Neuro-Psychiatric Center had exposed him to many people in mental health crisis—people who did not have the money or time to devote to seeing an analyst multiple days a week but who also didn't qualify for welfare. David saw this as a huge issue. These people needed help too, but no one was offering it.

So in 1958, at 31 years of age, David opened the nonprofit North Nassau Mental Health Center in Manhasset, Long Island. By this time, his family had moved to Oyster Bay, so while it was about an hour away from his other office in Manhattan, the clinic was only a short drive from home. The aim of this voluntary facility was to offer care at a low rate to people in need. As it wasn't beholden to governmental funding, North Nassau also had the capability to experiment with more holistic approaches than were generally considered at the time.

In the beginning, the clinic was open only in the evenings and on weekends to accommodate the rest of David's busy schedule. He attracted psychologists, psychiatrists, therapists, and social workers to the practice by offering them clients during times of the day when they normally wouldn't be seeing clients. Even though they charged less at North Nassau, the extra income was useful to most practitioners. This was also convenient for the clients, many of whom worked full days at jobs themselves.

LIFE OUTSIDE THE CLINIC

In 1960, Sally and David were divorced. The collapse of their marriage was due to a variety of issues, including David's addictions and his intense focus on his career, neither of which left very much time for him to be a family man.

Not long thereafter, he met Margaret Phelan, and they were soon married. With her exuberant native New Yorker personality and sense of humor, she was a great fit with David. Through this marriage, David gained a stepdaughter, Kathleen, who was about 10 years old. David adored Kathleen.

Also in 1960, David's dear sister, Sally-Claire, passed away. After several rounds of surgery, she went into a diabetic coma and died two days before turning 40. Her life being cut short was the first of several such losses for David, and it affected him greatly. What made her so afflicted, and was there anything that could have been done?

He was convinced of a connection between the body and mind, later even writing that "in order to facilitate healing, it is essential to understand the relationship between the body, the mind, and the spirit,"[1] an idea that was quite ahead of its time. David wanted to relieve suffering for as many people as he possibly could.

Also around 1960 (quite the time!), David met Bill Wilson, who had co-founded Alcoholics Anonymous almost 30 years previously. While David's addiction is covered in the next chapter, Wilson was instrumental in the direction North Nassau took, as you'll see in a few pages.

By this time, David's atheism had softened, or at least changed direction. David now considered himself an agnostic, meaning that he didn't believe or disbelieve in a higher power. The only thing he believed was that human experience was incapable of proving God's existence either way. What was unknowable was just that. David wasn't going to have faith in either the absence or existence of God without proof.

ADVENTURES IN ORTHOMOLECULAR MEDICINE

The term *schizophrenia* was coined in 1900 by Swiss psychiatrist Eugen Bleuler. Before that, it had been seen as demonic possession or untreatable madness. By the 1950s, it was considered a progressive biological condition that could be treated, though up to that point, it had mostly been dealt with through institutionalization, insulin coma therapy, Metrazol shock, electroconvulsive therapy, or surgery such as frontal lobotomy. Most schizophrenic patients ended up in institutions and never came out.

Antipsychotic drugs began being manufactured in the 1950s, but along with this progress in psychopharmacology, there was a parallel movement called orthomolecular medicine. This form of alternative medicine studied the effects of nutrition and aimed to restore health through dietary supplements. Proponents of this method believe that the chemicals found in vitamins and other naturally occurring substances were already present in the body; it was just their imbalance or deficiency that caused illness or disease.

Some doctors weren't just interested in treating psychosis; they also wanted to figure out why it affected some people and not others. Dr. Humphry Osmond and Dr. Abram Hoffer believed that a naturally occurring compound in the body, adrenochrome, might be the toxic agent causing schizophrenia. Adrenochrome is a byproduct of adrenalin that, in excess, causes cardiac dysfunction, hallucinations, and thought process disruptions.

The pair of doctors believed that an excess or build-up of adrenochrome in the body could cause schizophrenia. Hoffer suspected that niacin, otherwise known as vitamin B3, which was a known antidote for LSD, would work the same on adrenochrome. Niacin was shown to protect the heart against stress by lowering cholesterol and decreasing the release of fatty acids when the body was under stress. This hypothesis continues to be disputed, but Hoffer was a proponent all his life, stating in a 1994 paper that niacin is a "safe and effective therapeutic agent in the treatment of the schizophrenias and several other psychiatric diseases."[2]

After David's journey to hell and back with addiction (see Chapter 5), he became interested in vitamin therapy. Bill Wilson had been experimenting in this realm since 1958, when he met Dr. Hoffer and learned about his research on niacin therapy to relieve cravings in alcoholics. Niacin helps the body turn food into energy and is crucial for the health of the nervous system, digestion, and skin. While most people get plenty of niacin from the foods they eat, some do not. In addition, the supplement is harmless to take in large quantities and is quite inexpensive, especially compared to many psychopharmacological drugs.

In 1966, Bill Wilson wrote David a letter about niacin treatment for alcoholics and how effective it had been for him. The year before, Wilson had conducted a trial with 30 AA members who were still suffering from the effects of cravings and other issues despite being sober. Within two months of taking B3 supplements, two-thirds were mostly free of their symptoms and feeling healthier than ever. To top that off, patients with schizophrenic symptoms were experiencing benefits as well. David—whose clinic had more than a dozen psychiatrists at this time, all of whom had many patients with these issues—was intrigued.

North Nassau Mental Health Center was one of the first clinics in the States to support this alternative form of medicine. Dubbed megavitamin therapy, David's team began using vitamin B3 to help alcoholic and schizophrenic patients in April 1966.

The general dose would be three grams daily of vitamin B3. For schizophrenics or alcoholics in an acute withdrawal stage, this might even be upped to 12 grams. There were very few side effects to even these massive doses. Some patients experienced persistent flushing or rashes, but that was avoided by slowly building up the dose. Occasional nausea was reported, but it could generally be stymied by an antiacid or cold skim milk.

Along with large doses of niacin, the patients were prescribed balanced low-sugar, low-carb meals and given exercise plans. David was not hesitant to mix traditional medicine into treatment plans when necessary, putting patients on medications for depression or other issues as needed. This holistic approach was basically unheard of at the time. David and his team felt that they had nothing to lose: the vitamin was safe, and if nothing else, it might improve the patients' health.

In addition, David felt it was particularly important for the patient to have access to open and honest support. Before admitting a patient, his team would administer the Hoffer-Osmond diagnostic test (HOD), a true/false questionnaire that helped "quantify perceptive errors in mentally ill patients"[3] so that they could claim diagnosis with more certainty and less error. Upon receiving the results, they would share them directly with the patient, whereas many other doctors at the time would only tell the family. Many patients and their families came to North Nassau with confusion and conflicting information from other doctors, and they were relieved by the straightforwardness of David's approach.

He also found that honesty would result in better cooperation from the patient, and tried to give them as much agency as possible so they would care more about the outcome. The patients were given the book *How to Live with Schizophrenia* by Hoffer and Osmond to read and encouraged to join support and recovery groups. As David wrote in a 1968 brief, "the patient's illness was approached as being primarily a medical problem with psychological and social consequences."[4]

Starting in April, they administered megavitamin therapy to 315 adult patients who had been diagnosed with schizophrenia, 70 of whom also suffered from alcoholism and 89 percent of whom had already had previous treatment or hospitalization. The overall improvement rate for those 315 patients was 71 percent. They based this rate on the patient's subjective statements, the family's observations, the psychiatrist's evaluations, and a decrease in the HOA score.

David also worked with Wilson on his influential vitamin B3 therapy booklets, which are still used today in AA. Years later, when Wilson was asked what he wanted to be remembered for at the end of his life, he said it was for his work with vitamin B3 as a treatment for alcoholism—that's how strongly he felt about it.

At the clinic, the results spoke for themselves. David began training other psychiatrists in this approach and screened all his new clients for nutritional deficiencies. In January of 1967, North Nassau and Brunswick Hospital sponsored a meeting in Amityville to present findings from over a dozen psychiatrists who had been using the B3 therapy for a significant period. The reports covered over 1,200 cases, with most favorable results for helping alcoholic and schizophrenic patients recover. David reported that since beginning this approach, his clinic was able to close their electroconvulsive shock unit—shock treatments were one of the major mainstream medical treatments for schizophrenia at the time.

For the next four years, North Nassau treated over 2,000 patients for schizophrenia, most of them successfully without other kinds of intervention.

David's stories about patients were endless. He recalled one patient, a nun, who came in with her Superior to see David about her alcoholism. In their appointment, as David was listening, he studied her, noticing that she wasn't speaking right. Her speech was slurring a bit, and she didn't quite seem to be wholly present. He found out that they had stopped off at a drugstore on their way over. The nun had purchased some cough syrup and tied it to the rope of her habit—she was drunk!

In another case, a man came into the clinic who was acting like a mad hatter. He seemed to talk to people who weren't there, couldn't have a clear conversation with the people who were, and generally seemed to not know what was going on. At first, David and his team thought he was completely crazy, though he had no previous issues with mental illness. After doing their thorough intake process, they found out the man's job was working with pesticides, and he had lead poisoning. They caught it early enough that David's team was able to cure him.

Things started getting bigger too. Linus Pauling, a two-time Nobel laureate, wrote a paper called "Orthomolecular Methods in Medicine" in 1967, coining the term *orthomolecular*. The next year, he published a more famous article in *Science*'s April issue titled "Orthomolecular Psychiatry." *Ortho* comes from the Greek meaning "straight," "right," or "correct," so the term literally means "right molecule." Despite backlash in the wider medical community, Pauling then co-founded, with Art Robinson, the Institute of Orthomolecular Medicine in 1973 (though it was later renamed the Linus Pauling Institute of Science and Medicine). By 1976, the Orthomolecular Medical Society would be founded. This later led to the 1994 registration of the International Society for Orthomolecular Medicine, and with the *Journal of Orthomolecular Medicine* now thriving, which began in 1967.

David's involvement in the field was also influential. He truly wanted to share the amazing results of megavitamin therapy with as many people as possible. With Hoffer, Osmond, and a few other doctors, plans were hatched to put together a volume collecting work from prominent advocates in the field. David was asked to be the editor of the book. He approached Linus Pauling to write a foreword, and he was so enthused by the idea that he ended up being a co-editor for the project.

The book, titled *Orthomolecular Psychiatry: Treatment of Schizophrenia*, was published in early 1973 by W. H. Freeman and Company. Though it is out of print now, the book remains a treasure trove of case studies, research findings, clinical procedures, and theoretical understandings of using orthomolecular medicine to treat schizophrenia, alcoholism, and drug addiction.

As an advocate for orthomolecular psychiatry, David was in the minority. Despite the overwhelming evidence and case studies that have proved vitamin B3 therapy useful for recovering addicts and patients suffering from schizophrenia, it was never accepted by mainstream medicine. This was partly because David and the other involved doctors were less interested in publishing papers and more interested in helping patients recover.

After the years he struggled silently with his own addiction, which is explored in the next chapter, David especially did not see the use of doing experiments where some people in need did not get the treatment that could help them simply to prove to other doctors the worthiness of the cure. Instead, he just implemented the therapy for everyone.

CHAPTER 5

THE COST OF ADDICTION

How did David become so open-minded in looking for a cure for addiction? And why was he so interested in helping patients with this particular illness? On the outside during the 1950s, David's life seemed to be going well. His practice was blossoming. He grew personally as an analysand of a prominent psychiatrist.

But David was also plagued by illness at this point in his life, suffering variously from hemorrhagic diverticulitis, which is generally not painful and causes blood to appear in the stool, and bleeding ulcers, which while treatable, often landed David in the hospital to get blood transfusions. He also suffered from addiction to both alcohol and other drugs.

ADDICTION TAKES A TOLL

In the 1930s, as David writes in *Power vs. Force*, alcoholism was thought of as a "hopeless, progressive disease"[1] that was incurable. For David, drugs and alcohol offered a kind of escape. The feeling of being drunk or stoned took him to a higher plane that felt similar to his brushes with enlightenment. It was a blissful, uninhibited place where things felt good and made sense. Alcohol blunts negative feelings and creates euphoria, giving the drinker an experience they want to re-create again and again.

The problem is that when one stops drinking, they experience withdrawal. While drinking may lessen emotional discomfort while one is drinking, the lows become much lower in between. In addition, the body becomes accustomed to the effects of alcohol, requiring higher consumption to get the same feeling. Basically, the more you drink, the more you need to drink. It has since been discovered that there is a genetic component to alcoholism, so, with both his parents suffering from the illness, the cards were stacked that he would too.

David first achieved sobriety in late 1962 with the help of a Twelve Step program. But by Christmas of the next year, he'd relapsed, and things got progressively worse. Without the stimulants, David was plunged into a state of excessive anxiety and fear, the transcending of which would become a cornerstone of his later work. For now, though, he was trapped in the sheer terror of it.

The Charles B. Towns Hospital located on Central Park West was founded in 1901 and was a rehabilitation clinic that accepted only alcoholics and drug addicts. While Towns's "cure" was supported by some physicians, Towns himself was not a doctor. But because the clinic had strong connections to Alcoholics Anonymous, David checked himself in in early 1963. He stayed there three times to no effect, even when a doctor told him that his drinking would kill him in just a few months.

FINDING THE LANGUAGE OF THE HEART

David had been a constant alcoholic for more than half his life, and it was catching up with him. Though he considered his alcoholism a curse and an illness, he was truly addicted and could not stay away from drinking.

Rowland Hazard III, an alcoholic, sought treatment from Carl Jung, who wasn't able to completely fix him. But Jung told him that "science had no answer for this problem, that something above and beyond human experience had to be sought, and that the answer would be found in spirituality."[2] Hazard joined a hugely popular evangelical movement called the Oxford Group that was dedicated to personal change. After devoting himself to their principles, he found himself cured.

Hazard passed on what he learned to a suffering friend called Ebby Thacher, who found it effective as well and told fellow alcoholic Bill Wilson, who helped to found Alcoholics Anonymous in 1935, that "his recovery was based on service to others, moral housecleaning, anonymity, humility, and surrendering to a power greater than oneself."[3]

Wilson wasn't interested in the religious nature of the cure and fell into a deep depression. He gave up completely. "At this point, he had the profound experience of an infinite Presence and Light and felt a deep sense of peace. That night, he was finally able to sleep, and when he awoke the next day, he felt as though he had been transformed in some powerful, indescribable way."[4] Wilson realized that spiritual didn't necessarily mean religious; he was in power and could choose his own conception of God.

David met Bill Wilson in 1960 and formed a mentorship with him. Wilson recommended that he check out Harry Tiebout. Tiebout was a psychiatrist with whom Bill had shared his early manuscript—what became the Twelve Steps of AA—in 1939. Tiebout was an innovative thinker, open to all kinds of ideas to help his patients at Blythewood Sanitarium in Greenwich, Connecticut, many of whom suffered from mental health conditions and alcoholism. He was a strong proponent of the then-new idea that alcoholism was a disease and not a moral failing, as many of the time believed. He also brought the Twelve Steps into the psychoanalytic realm, bridging Freudian-based theory and AA concepts to guide recovery.

David saw Tiebout for analysis in the early '60s, with a focus on treating his alcoholism and related conditions through an understanding of the ego. Tiebout's road to recovery was formed on the basis of the big Ego, which remains inflated into adulthood due to issues of the psyche. The "act of surrender" was the only way to defeat the Ego according to Tiebout, an idea incorporated straight from AA's Christian--based faith teachings. As Tiebout wrote, "If and when he surrendered, he quit fighting, could admit he was licked, and could accept that he was powerless and needed help. If he did not surrender, a thousand crises could hit him and nothing would happen. The need to induce surrender became the new therapeutic goal."[5]

Tiebout's writing often comes across as more spiritual than medical, and he was able to combine psychoanalytic study with the more theologically based AA concepts to great effect. Both Tiebout and Alcoholics Anonymous would not only influence David's work with patients but also the formation of his own ideology later in life. "AA does not subscribe to any particular ethic, has no code of right and wrong or good and bad, and avoids moral judgments. AA does not try to control anyone, including its own members. What it does instead is chart a path."[6]

A SPIRITUAL PATH

While David could see that Bill and others had truly been cured by AA, he was in a state of crisis. He was agnostic, and therefore could not believe in some kind of higher power as AA required. David vehemently believed that there were no unknowables, that everything could be verified through actual, physical experience. So he began searching.

He researched a variety of alternative religious movements, including the Science of Mind teachings. Originally known as Religious Science, Dr. Ernest Holmes created this frame through a synthesis of the universal ideas that he found were available across all religions. He viewed religion simply as "a source of wisdom for revealing the Truth about the seemingly unknown forces that shape our universe."[7] This appealed to David because it didn't leave a vengeful or all-knowing God figure at the helm. Instead, each person participated in a co-creation of their own life.

In addition, "Buddhism was attractive because it avoided the use of the term 'God.'"[8] Of the many branches of Buddhism, David was drawn to Zen Buddhism, which became popular post-war due to counterculture acceptance of the peaceful ideals and the pursuit of enlightenment.

Zen began booming in the Western world: D. T. Suzuki translated Zen texts into English, making them more accessible, Shunryu Suzuki (no relation) founded the San Francisco Zen Center in 1962, and Alan Watts, an English theologian, wrote popular books explaining the practice. What drew David to Zen was that it was less of a religion and more of a pragmatic, practice-oriented mindfulness and inner searching. There is no dogmatic scripture or ritual in Zen.

He began learning Zen techniques, most specifically zazen, or seated meditation, which is the basis of Zen. Sitting in an upright posture in silence, being present in the moment, and noticing breath are the basics of this simple yet far-from-easy practice. David scrupulously meditated for an hour in the morning and an hour at night. But it wasn't helping his anxiety or his drinking.

David found himself on the edge of death, constantly depressed and as if he were living in a huge, dark hole from which there was no escape. On January 10, 1965, he contemplated leaving the body. But something beyond his despairing state stopped him.

Since his intention had been to find out the truth at all costs, he entered an intense meditative state, which cast him into utter despair and even "to the depths of hell in timeless dimensions of eternal agony in which one is forever cut off from the Light."[9] He sensed an endless, dark, terrifying isolation all around him, and even death could not be an escape. He experienced only silence and believed that this must be some kind of hell. He was beyond hope, immersed wholly in dread for a period that felt infinite. In complete despair and unending dread, David recalled that:

> From within, a silent voice cried out, "If there is a God, I ask him to help me," then I went into oblivion. When I regained awareness, there had been a major transformation. There was no longer any identification with a personal physical body. It walked around and did all the things it was supposed to do, but I stood in an energy field that was infinite. The power and dimension of the field were beyond description. It held me in absolute safety; it was like a rock. At the same time, it

was exquisitely soft and gentle. Its exquisite gentleness and softness held me in its infinite, loving embrace.[10]

When David came back to awareness, he found that:

The appearance of the world had changed and was dramatically transformed. It was now a silent, unified Oneness, magnificent in its brilliance that shone forth the Divinity of all existence. It magnified a single remaining discordant disparity—the persistence of a personal sense of a self as the core of one's life and existence. It was clear that this also had to be surrendered to the Presence. Then the fear of real death arose as terror. But with the terror also came the knowingness of an instruction from Zen Buddhism: "Walk straight ahead, no matter what—all fear is illusion."[11]

The necessity to abandon and surrender the identity of self as the source of one's existence was a powerful knowingness. The will to live, the seeming core of life itself, was then surrendered to God, followed by a few moments of terrifying agony and then the experience of death itself. This was unlike bodily death where one finds oneself suddenly free and looking at the body lying there, which had happened several times previously. No, this is the first and only time that death can be experienced. The finality of the death was overwhelming. At last, the agony was over and was replaced by splendor and magnificence—infinite stillness, silence, and the peace of profound Infinite Love. The mind was dumbfounded and overwhelmed with awe. It then became silent and disappeared.

Henceforth, only the Presence prevailed and all emerged autonomously without a personal will or motivation. The condition was a permanent replacement of the personal self—a silent, universal, timeless Presence by which the totality of Allness replaces any prior states of consciousness or the presumption of a personal self or "I."[12]

David saw only a state of ultimate Oneness beyond time, space, or definition, where "all things are interconnected and in communication and harmony by means of awareness and by sharing the basic quality of the essence of existence itself."[13] He was no longer a separate being, a self, an "I."

David's experience, which he called the Infinite Presence, instantly cured him of any desire for drugs or alcohol. He never experienced another craving and never imbibed again. Though he was severely addicted at this point, he had begun experimenting with drugs and alcohol because they brought him to a place that reminded him of that moment in the snowbank. But he didn't need help anymore; that experience arose all on its own.

RECOVERY AND THE PATH AFTER

It took him most of 1965 to understand and begin living comfortably with this new consciousness. He only ever spoke of it to Margaret, but she never really understood what he had gone through or why he felt it had changed him so drastically. She was pleased that he stopped drinking and taking drugs, and that was enough for her.

The main issue for David was that the things that used to matter just didn't anymore. He felt fully transformed on the inside, but on the outside, he looked the same as ever. He tried to go on with each day, looking for ways to motivate himself to deal with the clinic and his other responsibilities.

This is what led David to his journey into orthomolecular psychiatry. He wasn't sure what to do with his new consciousness, but he decided he could throw himself fully into helping people.

A critical component of recovery that David learned from Bill Wilson was community. Emphasizing that wellness was not just a physical thing but also crucially had mental, emotional, and spiritual components, David used the tenets of the Twelve Steps and applied them not only to his alcoholic patients but his schizophrenic ones as well. He even co-founded, with Father Joe, a Long Island chapter of Schizophrenics Anonymous (SA) that expanded so rapidly it had to be broken up into two groups, each of which had over 60 members by 1968.

Father Joe, a philosophy professor and alcoholic-schizophrenic with a lifelong depressive history, was one of the patients David had treated in 1966. He was initially treated with three grams of niacin, which was eventually raised to nine grams. He experienced a full recovery and even reported feeling more energetic than he ever had before. Fordham University, where he taught, then sponsored a panel that fall where David, Osmond, Hoffer, and other physicians spoke about B3 therapy in front of several hundred medical professionals, social workers, and others. It was the first time in the States that niacin therapy was put on public review.

Father Joe wanted to help others who were suffering like he had been. As he wrote, "The SA's program of recovery is based on the principles of AA's recovery program—plus medical treatment and strict adherence to certain simple health rules."[14] Members would, for the first time, learn how to understand and be in charge of their diagnosis. They were in community with others who suffered similarly, learning they were not alone and that there was a path to recovery.

They had access to halfway houses, such as Gateposts, which David sponsored and connected patients to. There is a chapter in *Orthomolecular Psychiatry* about Gateposts, which was the first orthomolecular halfway house in the United States. There was also a day activity center established with the help of St. George's Church and the Long Island Schizophrenic Association, and access to a family service social work agency to help support recovery. This community-based method of recovery was dubbed the Dr. Hawkins–Father Joe model.

David wrote about the model in 1977 that, in part, its success could

> be ascribed to the fact that we have filled a vacuum. Ours is the first treatment system which has established openness and honesty with patients and their families as a fundamental basis of operation. We were the first to have open public discussion of the disease of schizophrenia and, of course, the first to establish organizations such as the Canadian Schizophrenia Foundation and the American Schizophrenia Association to deal directly with this disease which, heretofore, like cancer, had been unmentionable.[15]

PART THREE

THE HIGH PASS
1979–1999

CHAPTER 6

ANOTHER TURNING POINT

In experiencing the Infinite Presence, David was living with a new consciousness, something that completely shifted his perception. While he had always been pulled to help and serve others, now he was the expression of love and healing and devoted his life to God by doing everything he could to relieve suffering and promote healing for as many people as possible. As David later put it:

> The person I had been no longer existed. . . . There was no personal will; the physical body went about its business under the direction of the infinitely powerful but exquisitely gentle Will of the Presence. In that state, there was no need to think about anything. All truth was self-evident and no conceptualization was necessary or even possible. At the same time, the physical nervous system felt extremely overtaxed, as though it were carrying far more energy than its circuits had been designed for.

It was not possible to function effectively in the world. All ordinary motivations had disappeared, along with all fear and anxiety. There was nothing to seek, as all was perfect. Fame, success, and money were meaningless. Friends urged the pragmatic return to clinical practice, but there was no ordinary motivation to do so.

There was now the ability to perceive the reality that underlay personalities: the origin of emotional sickness lay in people's belief that they were their personalities. And so, as though of its own, a clinical practice resumed and eventually became huge.[1]

This change greatly affected David and every aspect of his life. It was clear to his family, friends, and colleagues that something was different about David now, though he wasn't able to articulate exactly what had happened until many years later. It also affected his ability to practice medicine, though he was eventually drawn back in by the great need of the patients who sought out his practice:

> I went into an incredible state and after that, I couldn't practice medicine for some time. But I then slowly went back after some period of time. What actually happened was, very severe cases came from all over the world. I eventually ended up with the biggest psychiatric practice in the United States, actually. Two thousand outpatients, a thousand new patients a year. I had fifty employees, twenty-six offices, laboratories, research laboratories, et cetera. And I had a huge hospital practice as well. And into the hospital came the worst possible cases, given up by everybody—hopeless.

And some incredible, just to witness them. They'd be wound up in wet sheets, brought in manacles, from Maryland or someplace, and this writhing body would be put on the floor. And then, they were instantly seen through the eyes, seeing the Self of the entity within this psychotic mess. Instantly, there was like a healingness. The healingness was of the Spirit within. And at that point, the entity within couldn't have cared less about the state of the mind/body. It like realized its own truth, and in that instant, there was a healing.[2]

His commitment to helping people meant that he was often paid less or not at all—and his generosity did not go unnoticed. Many patients would give him other goods, such as homemade goods and meals. What mattered to David was that people got better, no matter what the prevailing institutional views of the time were. "My dedication to my patients was that I felt that my responsibility to God was to utilize everything I felt was helpful to the patient and not worry about my colleagues' approval—that in the end, I'll be answerable to Divinity for what I did with my gifts," David later said.[3]

David always took the point of view that he was treating a person—a unique individual with their own past, issues, dreams, and journey. Helping a patient was never just about the issue at hand and what the textbook said about a cure. A true and lasting fix would be one that was individualized, one that took into account every aspect of that person: body, mind, emotions, and spirit. He also treated all patients equally. A wealthy patient was just as deserving as one who was struggling to get by. Having been down in the trenches himself, he never looked down on people who were struggling with addiction or other issues. He simply wanted to help.

ANSWERS OUTSIDE THE BOX

A common issue in the late '60s was psychedelic drug overdoses, and David was involved in a service assisting people who were experiencing psychotic delusions or paranoia due to improper use of LSD. Lysergic acid diethylamide, the mind-bending marvel also known as LSD, is like a vivid rollercoaster for the brain, sending perception, cognition, and mood on a wild ride. When a person ingests LSD, it interacts with serotonin receptors, and suddenly, reality takes a vibrant detour. Colors explode, visuals get trippier than a kaleidoscope, and time warps into a fantastical journey. Emotions amplify, and users might feel intimately connected with the cosmos or witness the boundaries of their ego blur and come into a higher realm of consciousness. Not every trip is a smooth ride, though; sometimes, the adventure takes a twist into challenging or frightening territories. With its kaleidoscopic effects, LSD offers an experience that's as unpredictable as it is dazzling—a technicolor exploration of the mind that many at the time were seeking, either as an escape from some challenging realities or as a way to see beyond the human experience.

Always interested in expanding his understanding of the world, David was not opposed to drug use, and he even tried LSD. From his personal experience and from working with his clients, he generally felt that issues arose when too much of a drug was taken or a dependence on it was developed. So, as with everything, David considered taking LSD a very serious business. He wasn't interested in it just as a recreational lark or a way to pass the time. He was after the truth, an awakening, a way to reach an understanding of a higher realm and purpose that some people seemed to find with the drug. After preparing for an extended period of time with fasting and meditation, he made sure an experienced friend would be there to guide him, and David took a carefully measured amount of LSD. He proceeded to go on a trip that echoed his previous spiritual experiences.

On the trip, he experienced being with a spiritual guide who kept him safe. They walked for a long time through a beautiful natural landscape, just watching, listening, and living with the nature around them. When they paused, the guide gave David a rose, and he saw the aliveness of the flower pulsating out of it with an ethereal beauty. He saw that it was breathing, in and out, in and out. It was so alive and beautiful.

Always on the lookout for ways to apply orthomolecular therapy, David had found in his own practice that large quantities of vitamin B3 could help end bad trips. When he got wind of an upcoming music festival called Woodstock that would take place in upstate New York, he decided to go and help out the LSD rescue service that he worked with. While many of the medical workers at the festival were using Thorazine, "a powerful antipsychotic that resolves a frightening drug experience much as a ballistic missile resolves a ground skirmish," David offered vitamin B3.[4] David and the rescue service helped about 400 people recover from bad trips at the legendary festival.

While at the festival, he met an older woman who had a house right there. It was a rural area and usually she would not see many people. The hordes of music lovers wandering around, most of them experiencing some kind of high, scared her to death. They were all around her house, sitting in hammocks, and it was unlike anything she'd ever experienced before. She was clearly overwhelmed and distraught. David approached her, and just through his presence, she calmed down and was able to see that the festival attendees weren't harmful at all.

Through his work treating patients with LSD, David had previously been connected with Dr. J. Ross MacLean, who purchased the Hollywood Hospital in New Westminster, Canada, in 1957 and began using LSD to treat "alcoholism, anxiety disorders, depression and rocky marriages. Success, they said, was in the 50 to 80 per cent range," and before closing in 1975, the hospital had recorded over 3,000 supervised trips.[5] This psychedelic psychiatry interested David very much, as the results aligned with what he'd been discovering as well.

David's tactics were seen as unusual at the time, but he'd never forgotten how his mother had readily looked outside of the hospital for a solution to his severe allergic reaction to poison ivy when he was 12. An alternative treatment had saved his life back then, and everything he'd learned since had only confirmed that a holistic approach was the only approach.

This led to a broadening of his view about what constituted medical care and led him to deeply investigate and try out other alternative forms of healing, including Zen modalities and orthomolecular psychiatry along with more traditional psychoanalysis and medication. He applied this view to his own medical care as well as his patients, as shown in the time he decided to try acupuncture:

> I was one of the first patients in the United States to have acupuncture. I had a hopeless, chronic, recurrent duodenal ulcer that was going to lead to the necessity for subtotal gastrectomy. It was in Washington, D.C., and it was scientifically very well observed. You had to bring X-rays and everything with you to prove your medical condition. At the conclusion of treatment,

> they repeated all the same diagnostics, such as x-rays. From the third treatment on, my chronic, recurrent, hemorrhaging duodenal ulcer was cured and never recurred in all these years. This was 50 years ago. Permanent long-term cure for something that I had for 25 years. I had psychoanalysis and everything to try and cure it. So it may not be scientific, but it works.[6]

There were other signs pointing him to keep looking for answers, though. In one case, he saw two different doctors prescribing the same vitamin therapy to different patients. The patients of the first doctor were more inclined to develop slight side effects like skin discoloration, while the patients of the second doctor had none at all. What was going on here, David wondered? Why did the second doctor have better results than the other? It was dawning on him that it all came down to consciousness. "The amount of side effects that a doctor's patients have depends on the consciousness of the doctor. It doesn't depend on the medicine."[7] The higher the level of consciousness of the doctor, the better the results.

As he later wrote in *Healing and Recovery*: "It is said that all diseases, illnesses, and human problems are physical, mental, and spiritual, but what does that really mean? As a physician for more than fifty years, I have learned about the physical aspects; as a psychiatrist, I have learned about the mental components; and in consciousness and spiritual research and experience, I have learned about the spiritual dimension."[8] By the early '70s, he had accomplished the physical and mental—though he was always on the lookout for new modalities—and had already started considering the spiritual. But he would soon itch for something more.

HIGH LIFE

Outside of work, David's life had vastly improved since his time growing up hand-to-mouth in a small, suburban Milwaukee home. By 1970, he had purchased 25 acres in Upper Brookville on Long Island, a highly affluent area that was originally home to wealthy movers and shakers like the Rockefellers and Vanderbilts. It was just 25 miles from Manhattan. Today, this area is home to multimillion-dollar homes, estates, and mansions.

David's main attraction in living in this area was privacy. He greatly valued time away from the hustle and bustle of the city, which was part of the reason why he initially moved to Long Island. He craved anonymity for himself and his family and always put a high priority on safety, especially since he'd had a few dangerous experiences with patients experiencing paranoia or delusions. Access to nature was also a must for David, and he could often be found roaming the undeveloped woods that bordered his land and went on for a hundred acres.

Always the jack-of-all-trades, David set about sketching plans for an estate on this land in the early 1970s. His influence was the French Normandy–style architecture that he'd seen in Europe and he designed a spacious and elegant estate where he, Margaret, and his three daughters, who were now teenagers, would live.

The estate was surrounded by tall, elegant trees that shaded the buildings and made it feel like a forested retreat. It was a beautifully green area that was quiet, with the neighbors spaced out for privacy. The buildings were all multi-story, featuring numerous steeply pitched gables and large windows that let in lots of light. Some of the windows featured stained glass recovered from historic churches. Some of the exterior walls were done in red brick on the bottom half, but most of them were a light-colored stucco. Distinctive to the Normandy style, dark brown decorative half timbering crisscrossed the exterior walls. Ivy crawled up the sides of the home and there was lush landscaping throughout.

After passing the two gatehouses and driving down a winding gravel road of nearly a mile, the main residence featured a brick courtyard and magnificent fountain out front, and the main entrance was located in a rounded tower with a cone-shaped roof. Inside the front door, a magnificent oak staircase wound up two flights. The rooms were bright and cozy, many of them with large wood-burning fireplaces that the family would cozy up beside in the winter. The rooms featured exposed wooden beams.

There were also five bedrooms, a massive four-car garage, a living room and library wing, a dining wing, a kitchen wing with a breezeway, and abundant outdoor gardens, including a vegetable garden that David could often be seen tending. Part of the Normandy aesthetic was that the building would appear to have developed over time, something that may have been especially intriguing to David and his constant search for new ideas and ways of thought.

Reading was instilled as a core value when he was a child, and David never lost his love of books. By this time, he'd amassed an extensive collection of books that included many medical texts and spiritual books as well as novels. The library, with over six thousand volumes, was a wondrous thing to behold, and David and his family spent many hours there. David used the large garage for many things. It had a studio above where David would tinker with his various projects—he was filled with ideas and always inventing a new kind of useful device. The girls loved to go roller skating in the garage, a skill that David taught them, among other things, including how to safely use guns.

He called the estate French Country, and it was located at 53 Mill River Road in Oyster Bay, New York. When he had it appraised in October 1976 for estate planning purposes, the market value of the home was $470,000, which in 2024 would be around $2.56 million. The buildings still stand today, though in 1995 he renovated the estate and extended the property, adding a 75-foot heated pool, large family room with cathedral ceilings, more bedrooms, and a large, manicured lawn. All the additions maintain the French style and elegance that David envisioned and created.

Living in this area, as he had since 1958, meant he was eligible to be part of influential social clubs and groups with wealthy industry leaders. For example, when David wanted to open North Nassau Clinic, there seemed to be endless bureaucratic red tape, paperwork, and issues. But David had an influential friend who used his family connection to make a call to the state licensing board, and almost overnight, he had a green light.

While David understood the importance and enjoyed the perks of being "one of the boys," he was never seduced by that ultra-rich lifestyle. He got his hands dirty when building his estate, helping out with masonry, stonecutting, and other building tasks along with design. Margaret got in on the work as well: she worked with pottery and had a kiln. She made the floor tiles for the house, so each tile was original and unique. David also opted to drive his reliable, unpretentious 1946 Packard convertible until he could not replace the parts for it anymore. As time passed, he became more and more disillusioned with the lifestyle that was expected by the people in these circles. Materialism never much appealed to David, and his spiritual experiences were making it clear that there was much more to learn.

EXPERIENCING LOSS

David did not remain close with either of his parents, who would both remarry two more times. Ramon quit the automotive industry and decided to get in touch with nature. He ran a successful tree farm, spending each day out in the sunshine, getting his hands dirty. After retiring for good, he moved to Oregon with his third wife, where David would visit every once in a while, so Ramon could spend time with his grandchildren. Ramon remained devoted to his faith and, on January 30, 1972, passed away while playing the organ at church from an aortic aneurysm. He truly went out doing what he loved.

David spent a lot of time wandering around in the untamed nature around his estate. It was a space where he would go to be fully alone, sinking into that deeper state of divine Presence and silent peace that he had to tamp down in order to exist and function in the everyday world. But here, surrounded by the soft murmurs of birds, the smell of dirt, and the sunlight peeking through the trees, he could enter a trance-like, meditative state, accessing a higher plane of being.

It was during one of these walks that he had a sudden knowing that his mother wasn't long for this world. He went back to the house and immediately got a plane ticket to Florida for the next day. Then he called to see how she was doing and found out that she was in the hospital with liver failure. The prognosis was grim. Though he hadn't remained close with his mother, he still felt a strong connection to her and immediately flew to Florida, where she lived with her third husband.

David had a lot of experience being around the dying, and he'd spent—and would continue to spend—lots of time with people in their final moments. He never felt it was something to be sad about; rather, when he psychically connected with them, he always sensed great relief and an outpouring of love. Death wasn't an ending; it was merely passage to the next state. It was the same with his mother. When he entered her hospital room, she was lying on the bed with many cords and tubes attached to her, keeping her alive. She was no longer conscious, but her body was holding on. Despite there having been very little communication between the two of them for many years, David felt a huge sense of relief from his mother when he entered her hospital room. He felt that she had known he was coming, and she had waited until her own son arrived at her side to truly die. "She had wanted me to experience the experience with her, and so I experienced that ever-expanding, infinite, absolute state of ecstasy as she went into that state."[9]

As David later wrote, "It is during life that one often feels alone and, at the moment of death, there is an absolute feeling of oneness and connectedness."[10] It was this feeling that he was able to tap into and experience alongside the dying, which solidified his belief that death was not the end. Being able to experience that ecstatic moment with his mother meant the world to David, even though the doctors and other hospital staff in the room were completely unaware of what was happening.

Knowing that the soul transcended death, of course, did not lessen the sting of grief. Around 1970, when his daughter Kathleen was in college, she discovered a lump on her neck that turned out to be Hodgkin's disease.

Hodgkin's disease, a form of lymphoma, profoundly affects individuals by targeting their lymphatic system, a vital component of the immune system. This cancer often manifests with painless swelling of lymph nodes, particularly in areas like the neck, underarms, or groin. Beyond the physical toll of the disease, Hodgkin's can bring about systemic symptoms such as fever, fatigue, unintended weight loss, and night sweats, deeply impacting a person's overall well-being. The disruption of the lymphatic system compromises the body's natural defense mechanisms, making individuals more susceptible to infections.

Though later in the 1970s, the treatment landscape for Hodgkin's disease would undergo significant changes, the implementation of combining chemotherapy, radiation therapy, and surgery to remove the lymphoma was all that was available to help Kathleen at the time. David and Margaret were there with Kathleen every step of the way, but the disease continued to progress despite the treatments. Kathleen, only 26 years old, passed away in early July of 1976.

Margaret was consumed by her grief and the trauma of losing her daughter, who was still so young and full of potential. That, and the fact that their relationship was already strained, meant that the marriage of David and Margaret didn't last much longer. David, also experiencing the loss of his stepdaughter, looked for spiritual answers to heal his mind and spirit. He devoured works on the subject, including Elisabeth Kübler-Ross's groundbreaking 1969 book, *On Death and Dying*.

Her heartrending death was a huge catalyst for the work that David would go on to do. While he felt grief at her passing because she was so young, he had the understanding that a person doesn't really die; they just transition to another plane. He was spurred on to finding a way to let go of the lower emotions, and much of his work later in life would revolve around understanding and unpacking emotional conditions like grief, anger, pain, fear, anxiety, and other internal crises so that they can be let go and transformed into positive feelings, emotional growth, and spiritual advancement.

It was around this time that he became less interested in orthomolecular psychiatry and began thinking about more of a personal health and spiritual quest. After all, though he'd been able to help so many people, he still suffered from a variety of chronic illnesses and physical ailments, many of which had plagued him for decades. These issues included Graves' disease, a collapsed lung, heart failure, a type of aviary tuberculosis, anasarca edema, hemorrhagic diverticulitis, bleeding ulcers, chronic migraine attacks, stress-related illnesses, eye issues (including astigmatism), earaches, sinusitis, skin issues, gout, hypoglycemia, high cholesterol, various gastrointestinal issues, Raynaud's syndrome, heart issues, colitis, debilitating allergies, and more.

To the outside world, he seemed a happy, successful man, but the truth was that physically, mentally, and spiritually, he was in need of a new way of life. At one point, David struggled with 27 diseases at the same time. He refused medical treatment, and yet, all the issues disappeared once he surrendered his life to God and began exploring the variety of the Human Potential Movement.

CHAPTER 7

A WORLD OF HUMAN POTENTIAL

David was always on the search for something more. Walking down the streets of New York City, he felt the world was filled with potential and he saw love everywhere—the perfection that was the innate beauty of all creation was all around, if only one would stop to see it. This story is one he later loved to tell:

> Each thing becomes a living sculpture, each thing is a sculpture. And after that the condition prevailed. Walking down an alley in New York City, I saw like an incredible painting by an impressionist, the garbage can all crooked over, like this. And the garbage all laying there. And, you see, you take an eggshell, it's an egg, you take an orange, and it's orange. You turn them all up and put them together and put them in a can, and now it's called garbage. It hasn't been becoming different than what it is, but its appearance is different.[1]

His spiritual experiences kept compiling, leading him to the undeniable fact that somewhere in the universe or deep in the psyche were answers to questions that hadn't even been asked yet, questions that were out beyond the limited scope of average human understanding. And he wanted to find them.

This was the quest to which he devoted the rest of the '70s, diving deep into any kind of new consciousness modality that struck his interest. This decade was a time of change; after the upheaval of the Vietnam War, people trusted the government less and wanted to become their own authority. David was not the only one searching for answers outside the norm, and he encountered a lot of unique modalities, some of which would become integral to the development of the Map of Consciousness®.

The Human Potential Movement was born out of this desire for meaning. This wide-reaching movement combined Eastern philosophy with Western psychology with an intent on self-improvement. Abraham Maslow, a psychologist most well-known for his hierarchy of needs, co-founded the American Association of Humanistic Psychology and popularized the theory of self-actualization, which he believed could be achieved if human needs are met in a specific order. Many different ideas spawned out of the Human Potential Movement, and David explored the techniques, modes of study, and self-actualization groups discussed in this chapter deeply during this time.

EST

Werner Erhard, considered by many to be the "father of self-help," developed what he called EST training in 1971. The training was about 60 hours in total, with two weekend--long workshops and evening sessions during the week to accommodate for work schedules. Participants would gather and spend upward of 15 hours each day in rigorous conditions that included no watches, no eating, no note-taking, no speaking unless called upon, and no bathroom breaks except at predetermined points during the day.

Through this strictness, Erhard's program broke people of the ways that they would normally try to avoid challenging situations. The idea of the program was to use Socratic-style interrogation—which could be quite harsh—to get participants outside of themselves so they could actually observe their own ingrained behavior and rote habits, and thus, begin to change them for the better.

David took this training in 1975, just at the beginning of the EST training program's massive boom in popularity, which would be worldwide in four more years. It may have appealed to him in part due to its similarity to Zen teachings, many of which were intended to trick the mind into becoming aware of itself and raising consciousness. David also connected with Erhard's idea that the things people are searching for, like happiness and success, come from within oneself, not from external things like jobs, money, or other people. It was predicated on the self: self-reliance, self-motivation, self-discipline. As David said:

> The purpose of Est was to get you off projecting blame and to own—to become empowered by owning—that it wasn't the traffic that made you late. If you were late to an Est meeting you had to stand outside the door and the trainer would ask you why you were late. You would say, "Well, I missed the bus." You would have to stand there and wait some more. "And the elevator was slow." Uh huh. "And the alarm didn't

go off." Uh huh. And finally, he, the attendee, said, "I chose to be late."

"Okay, you may come in now."

You had to own yourself, that some aspect of you decided that. Some aspect. You didn't set two alarms, you didn't set a back up to make sure, et cetera. . . . If you did Est, you were successful for you now had the courage to own your own decisions and take responsibility.[2]

The main takeaway he got from Erhard's method was to recognize that the emotions that might come up around a specific situation, conversation, or person were not always related to that moment. They were more likely habitual feelings or patterns based on old hurts or traumas that arose as a defensive mechanism.

The honesty and laid-bare nature of the program were highly influential to David, though his adaptation of some of the ideas would smooth out the hard, blunt edges and substitute warm humor instead.

INTEGRITY TONE SCALE

Psychologist Vern Black was an EST trainer who created a tool mapping developmental levels based on what he called their integrity. Drawing on his EST background, Black considered his tool "a road map to the mind" that was meant to help the user see that it wasn't the circumstances of their life that determined their point of view but rather their reaction to those circumstances.[3] Black's model, called the Integrity Tone Scale, had 10 levels of integrity: Disloyalty, Adversary,

Uncertainty, Detriment/Responsible, Non-Existence, Danger, Emergency, Normal, Abundance, and Empower/Source.

"The Integrity Tone Scale can be used to locate your experience and another's experience of any given situation and assist you in changing that experience at choice."[4] By changing your mind, emotions, and reactions, you can change your circumstances and begin to operate at a higher level of integrity. In the chart, each level of integrity also has an emotion, attitude, point of view, apparent result, and commendment to expand (the latter of which gave users some ideas on how to move up to the next level of integrity). Each of these columns offer descriptors that help illuminate each level. For example (as laid out in the Integrity Tone Scale in Black's second self-published book, *Love Me? Love Yourself*):

State of Integrity	Emotion	Attitude	Point of View	Apparent Result	Commendment to Expand
Abundance	Exhilaration Aesthetic	Gratefulness Cherishing Ardor Enchantment	Welcome	Devotion	Be devoted Economize Study for even more results Strengthen the abundance

The style and organization of Black's Integrity Tone Scale would be a large part of the foundation for the Map of Consciousness®. (Interestingly, L. Ron Hubbard also seemed to have been influenced by the Integrity Tone Scale in his creation of the Emotional Tone Scale of Scientology, though his version is meant to give users the ability to predict the behavior of others rather than insight on how to change themselves for the better.)

THE SEDONA METHOD

Lester Levenson was a sick man. In 1952, he was so sick, in fact, that after a coronary, his doctors were certain that he would die. But he wasn't ready to give up. He got to thinking that the high-stress demands of his job as a physicist and the demands of living in society were part of the problem—he was carrying around all these pent-up feelings of fear, inadequacy, stress, and so on. He didn't have anything left to lose, so he decided to let all of that go. He discovered that "we are all unlimited beings, limited only by the concepts of limitation that we hold in our minds."[5] After developing a system of releasing his negative feelings, he miraculously recovered fully three months later. He then realized that most people go around feeling that life is difficult and stressful, and he began working with groups of people to share what he'd done to turn his life around.

While initially it was known as Mind Freedom or the Mind Freedom Technique, it became known as the Sedona Method and was formalized by Levenson in 1973. It focuses on the idea of "letting go" or "releasing" emotions and ideas, teaching practitioners to focus on *how* they process their experiences and emotions, allowing them to consciously choose what they feel or don't feel, have or don't have. This can be applied to physical pain as well as emotional pain, and the concept can be adapted for use in any area of life.

The basic technique, which can be used at any time when feeling a strong emotion, involves asking yourself a set of questions: *Could you let it go? Would you? And when?* These questions help lead the questioner to consciously realize what emotions they are needlessly gripping so they can just let them go. The method was based around six steps:

1. You must want freedom more than you want approval and control.
2. You must accept that you can do the method and be free.
3. See each feeling as either wanting approval or wanting to control and release the want of approval or the want to control.
4. Make it constant. Use all feelings when alone or with people.
5. If you are stuck, let go of wanting to change the stuckness.
6. Each time you use the method, you feel a bit freer and happier. If you do this continually, you will continually feel freer and happier.[6]

On a version of these steps that David kept among his personal papers, he had annotated a note about step six: "wanting to get to 'top of the mountain' where oneness and the universe is." That oneness—the idea he'd been chasing for so long, was closer than he thought.

The technique also utilized the Scale of Action in Emotions that used nine categories of emotion: Apathy, Grief, Fear, Lust, Anger, Pride, Courageousness, Acceptance, and Peace. These were arranged in a pyramid with Apathy at the bottom and Peace at the top.[7] (Originally, there were six emotions; Lust, Pride, and Peace were added later on.) Learning how to release the lower emotions allowed a practitioner to experience greater states of the higher emotions, Courageousness, Acceptance, and Peace.

Since its conception, the Sedona Method has been used by countless individuals for self-improvement as well as Fortune

500 companies who showed sales increases due to the tactics. David took a two-weekend workshop on the Sedona Method in New York in 1976 from Virginia Lloyd, where he got to meet Lester Levenson. Part of what she taught included the nine fundamental emotional states: Apathy, Grief, Fear, Lust, Anger, Pride, Courageousness, Acceptance, and Peace. These levels would be instrumental in David's Map of Consciousness®. Lloyd would go on to publish a book on the topic in 1986 titled *Master Your Emotions.*

Initially, David was unsure that the Sedona Method was for him. As both a physician and a lifelong intellectual, he was used to living in his head, dealing solely with thoughts and logic. But one thing that the workshop stressed was that belief wasn't necessary, just the willingness to give it a try. Lloyd, Levenson, and the other advocates of this method taught it this way because they were certain that the results would speak for themselves.

David remained open to the ideas presented in the workshop. Through the teachings, he began to realize that he often went through the business of his days with a detachment from the emotional side of things. He had been repressing and resisting his feelings for so long, he barely noticed that he didn't feel them anymore. While this was useful for making quick decisions during emergencies or guiding patients during therapy, it was no way to live. He even thought that it might be the root of some of his long-lasting physical ailments. Connecting the releasing method with his burgeoning ideas about consciousness being crucial to true inner healing, David started experimenting with the techniques and found them amazingly productive. He simply let go of his resistance to feeling the physical or emotional pain and then let go of the pain itself.

During this time, he was struggling with ailments that were mostly stress-related but affecting him physically. A gastrointestinal illness was so intense, he was scheduled to have surgery for it. His diverticulitis was back stronger than ever, with added hemorrhaging. He knew that these conditions were being exacerbated by the lower emotional states, but he hadn't been able to get past them. "I put all the teachings I had learned thus far on the line—I made the decision: either this stuff works, or I check out."[8] He was desperate, but that also meant he put his whole self into this life-or-death experiment.

It began to work.

His first experiment with releasing his gastrointestinal pain was so effective, he cancelled the surgery. His diverticulitis went away—he simply released it. David loved to tell the story of when he was chopping wood just before Thanksgiving and broke his foot. He decided not to get a cast, instead applying the Sedona Method and letting go of the pain. Just a few weeks later, in time for Christmas, he was walking without a limp—and even dancing! He found that he could change the very physical and chemical makeup of his body just by changing his mind.

He went on to take the advanced training in the Sedona Method and this technique of shifting the consciousness would continue to be something he used for the rest of his life, becoming integral to the foundation of his own teachings, as shown throughout the book *Letting Go*:

> The mind, with its thoughts, is driven by feelings. Each feeling is the cumulative derivative of many thousands of thoughts. Because most people throughout their lives repress, suppress, and try to escape from their feelings, the suppressed energy accumulates

and seeks expression through psychosomatic distress, bodily disorders, emotional illnesses, and disordered behavior in interpersonal relationships. The accumulated feelings block spiritual growth and awareness, as well as success in many areas of life.[9]

David's letting go technique "is a pragmatic system of eliminating obstacles and attachments. It can also be called a mechanism of surrender," and it works on all levels of the self: physical, behavioral, interpersonal relationships, and consciousness.[10] Without the Sedona Method, David never would have developed his discoveries about consciousness.

He was so impressed with the method that he even wound up being featured in *The Sedona Method* subscriber magazine in September 1979, about two years after he started using it. The article calls him the "father of orthomolecular psychiatry" and quotes him as saying: "I was impressed with the clarity, simplicity and brilliance of The Method and the context in which it was presented. I was also impressed by its purity; it is uncontaminated by the introduction of any new belief systems, and is very efficient compared to the slow, tedious method of psychotherapy."[11] He went on to say:

> My life became more positive as I released many things. The grief reaction to my daughter's death disappeared. The capacity to love others increased to the point of being able to feel love toward anyone who came into my life, even the most severely provocative and disturbed patients. My professional work became even more proficient; I found I could work half as many hours and earn twice as much.

I had had several physical ailments, and the week after taking the course was scheduled for surgery. But within a few days after beginning to release, the surgical condition disappeared and never re-appeared. My other physical problems cleared up. I believe these good effects are due to stress reduction brought about by using The Method.

MUSCLE TESTING

Also known as applied kinesiology, this alternative wellness therapy sparked David's interest immediately, as it seemed to combine his two main areas of interest: physical medicine and energetic medicine.

Dr. George Goodheart pioneered the idea of *applied kinesiology*, which works similarly to a knee-jerk or nerve test, which is when a doctor taps on a patient's knee to elicit a kicking response. This test shares information not about the knee, but about how the brain and spinal cord are functioning. The applied kinesiology test differs in that it tests muscles instead of nerves. The basic technique for testing a shoulder muscle, for example, includes the patient extending their arm and the practitioner pressing down on the arm while the patient presses up. If the patient is able to easily resist, the muscles are strong. In this way, imbalances can be found in the body.

Though initially intriguing, scientific testing and evidence did not support the claim that muscle testing could accurately diagnose physical conditions. But there was something there. John Diamond was a physician focused on holistic healing methods, and he was interested in the link between acupuncture meridians (the paths in the body through which energy flows) and our emotions. He built on Goodheart's ideas, refining them into a technique he called *behavior kinesiology*. This branch was based on his discovery that, beyond simply responding to physical stimuli, muscles would respond to intellectual and emotional stimuli as well.

David attended a seminar held by Diamond and was impressed by what he saw. The way that Diamond presented the test is summarized in *Power vs. Force*:

1. Have the subject stand erect, right arm relaxed at his side, left arm held out parallel to the floor, elbow straight. (You may use the other arm if you wish.)

2. Face your subject and place your left hand on his right shoulder to steady him. Then place your right hand on the subject's extended left arm just above the wrist.

3. Tell the subject you are going to try to push his arm down as he resists with all his strength.

4. Now push down on his arm fairly quickly, firmly, and evenly. The idea is to push just hard enough to test the spring and bounce in the arm, but not so hard that the muscle becomes fatigued. It is not a question of who is stronger, but of whether the muscle can "lock" the shoulder joint against the push.[12]

A simple version of this test is to ask objectively yes or no questions or specific statements while muscle testing and see if the muscle stays strong (a positive or yes response) or goes weak (a negative or no response). This can also be used to understand the effects of negative energies; for example,

David found that having participants stare at fluorescent lights would make them go weak.

For David, this technique clearly revealed some underlying truth. Diamond believed that muscle testing was identifying what was going on at an unconscious level—which is where most of our processing takes place. But perhaps it went even further than that. David was already pondering whether it was a response to the universal life energy that flowed around and through all of us all the time. As he later said:

> When I first saw kinesiology, I had already gone into that infinite paradigm we call nonlinear, and which religiously is called Presence of God. So, when I first saw it, I was already seeing it from a different paradigm of reality. The whole audience was within the linear Newtonian domain. What they saw was a local phenomenon and what I saw was a non-local phenomenon. We both witnessed the same event. To me it was obviously the non-local answer coming from the nature of consciousness itself. And the rest of the audience saw it as the reaction of the body's physiology. . . . But it was very clearly a nonlinear, impersonal response. It has nothing to do with the questioner, it has nothing to do with the person who was being the subject. And it was obviously the connection between the invisible nonlinear domain, and the consciousness of mankind as it expresses itself through the nervous system. So instantly what I saw was infinite, non-local, impersonal, and was a response of consciousness itself to the presence of Truth.[13]

So, it opened then, that kinesiology could be used beyond the linear and beyond the local, and in experimenting with it over many years now, we found that we had a means of directly accessing a field called "consciousness," which is again, very iffy to people who live in the Newtonian paradigm of reality. The "consciousness" in that definition is whether you're awake or asleep.[14]

David considered muscle testing "the 'wormhole' between two universes—the physical world and the world of the mind and spirit—an interface between dimensions. In a world full of sleepers lost from their source, here was a tool to recover, and demonstrate for all to see, that lost connection with the higher reality."[15] It would later become a staple in his work as he created the Map of Consciousness® and tested the levels of various places, statements, people, things, and much more.

David noted about applied kinesiology in an interview that "it was quite interesting that the negative energy made the person go weak, and the positive energy made them go strong. The source of the energy did not have to be in physical contact with the body, just in proximity. So, it was obvious that we were dealing with an energy field and that somehow the human nervous system, autonomic system, was able to discern the difference."[16]

This was yet another connection, another link in the chain, leading to David's understanding of the energy of all things and how the levels of consciousness can be affected energy. Later on, when he was on the lecture circuit, David would test the audience to show them the effectiveness of this technique:

In audiences of 1,000 people, 500 envelopes containing artificial sweetener would be passed out to the audience, along with 500 identical envelopes containing organic vitamin C. The audience would then be divided up and would alternate testing each other. When the envelopes were opened, the audience reaction was always one of amazement and delight when they saw that everybody had gone weak in response to the artificial sweetener and strong in response to the organic vitamin C.[17]

It never failed. Even when the conscious mind of the participant was completely unaware of the truth, the body would still respond accurately.

A COURSE IN MIRACLES

Around this same time in 1978, David discovered *A Course in Miracles* (ACIM) and became a student and member of the training program. This spiritual self-study program has many parallels to Alcoholics Anonymous, focusing on achieving peace, happiness, and inner healing through the practice of forgiveness and shifting perceptions from fear to love. This thought system has curious origins; it is claimed to have been "scribed" by psychologist Helen Schucman "through a process of inner dictation that she identified as coming from Jesus."[18]

Interestingly, Schucman considered herself an atheist and thought that she might be going crazy during the process. Her assistant, William Thetford, encouraged her to listen to the voice she heard that kept telling her in 1965, "This is a course in miracles. Please take notes." Though reluctant, Schucman ended up taking down notes over the next seven and a half years, which Thetford typed up into what would become the Course.

The Course is separated into three volumes: the Text, the Workbook for Students, and the Manual for Teachers. The Text offers the theory and main explanations for the idea of the Course, while the Workbook for Students is where the reader begins doing the work. It contains 365 lessons that the reader can go through at their own pace. Though the language of the Course is filtered through a lens of Christianity, the spiritual ideas that it contains are not beholden to any belief system (a similarity it has with AA).

David heard about ACIM very early, when there were only about 25,000 copies available in print. The Foundation for Inner Peace was the first publisher of the Course, and they still offer the only complete and authorized version free on their website. They have also since translated it into 27 languages. Similar to the other modalities David was exploring, ACIM emphasizes a shift in perspective and the idea that one is only subject to what they hold in their mind. What the mind perceives, the body believes, as the saying goes, and David began consciously deciding that he would cancel his ingrained perceptions that did not support his highest physical or mental well-being.

David found the ACIM method groundbreaking. He invested in 50 copies of the Course and would hand them out to family, friends, staff, patients, and anyone else who seemed in need. In experimenting with applied kinesiology at his clinic, David realized that his volunteers who were studying ACIM did not react to the negative energies in the same way that other people did. "In fact, they didn't go weak to any of the stimuli that made ordinary people go weak. I became curious about what is different about them; this led me into the study of consciousness."[19] Along with studying the Course himself, David began using ACIM therapeutically to help his patients recognize the unconscious beliefs that were holding them back.

This was a modality already in use by psychiatrist Gerald Jampolsky, who had founded the International Center for Attitudinal Healing in California after his own life-changing experience with *A Course in Miracles*. What he dubbed attitudinal healing was based on the idea that it is one's own ingrained thoughts, judgments, and beliefs that cause us to have negative emotions, not external things like the people around us or situations that happen to us. By focusing on changing one's own attitude—by letting go of fear (a combination of the Sedona Method and ACIM)—one can find true inner peace and health.

David met up with Jampolsky to learn more about his center, and he soon opened the Attitudinal Healing Center of Long Island in his Manhasset clinic. Using these methods, many patients saw improvements, even finding that their conditions disappeared altogether. In David's words:

> We saw people with every illness on the face of the Earth go into remission or recover. And that started these Attitudinal Healing Centers, which were based on that group, a spiritual approach to chronic and incurable illnesses. Jerry Jampolsky started one out in Tiburon. He wrote *Love Is Letting Go of Fear*. Jampolsky brought his whole staff back east, where I had a big clinic. We started the second Attitudinal Healing Center in New York. And there we did also see every kind of illness known to mankind remit. And this particular body, which was afflicted with all kinds of disasters in my thirties, it slowly remitted from a whole lot of these disasters, including the ability to see.[20]

Though the Long Island center was dissolved in 1993, Attitudinal Healing International has centers all over the world and continues to grow.

OUT-OF-BODY EXPERIENCES

Robert Monroe was a writer and radio producer and director who was interested in human consciousness studies. After going through several spontaneous out-of-body experiences, he expanded his research, eventually building the Monroe Institute in Virginia, to discover practical techniques to attain and enhance this altered, higher state of consciousness. Monroe's first book, *Journeys Out of the Body*, was published in 1971, and it caught David's attention, as he, too, had had an out-of-body experience, though he hadn't known what to call it at the time.

This had been back when he was in psychotherapeutic analysis with Lionel Ovesey. David wound up in the hospital due to his ongoing issues with hemorrhagic diverticulitis and bleeding ulcers and was on the edge of death. He recalls lying there, in immense pain, and then having a strange lifting feeling enter his body. Suddenly, he was hovering over himself, his consciousness seemingly divorced from his physical form, and he could look down and see his body below.

> There I was, in space, in a perfect body that was transparent and ethereal. It was weightless, yet I had all my faculties. I could think, reason, see, and hear. I looked down at the physical body that was lying the bed about eight to ten feet below me, and it looked like it was about to expire. There I was, outside the physical body, looking down at it, aware that that which I really am is something other than the physical body.[21]

He felt a deep knowing in that moment that he was more than his body, but he also felt that it wasn't time yet for him to leave his body, so he allowed himself to float back into the form lying prone on the bed.

That was the late 1950s, and David had never heard the terms "near-death experience" or "out-of-body experience" before. When he discussed it with Ovesey, they chalked it up to some kind of toxic stress reaction to the immense pain he was in and didn't speak of it further. But when he came upon Monroe's book two decades later, he was immediately transported back to that time with the striking realization that he had gone through an out-of-body experience. It validated the ideas about consciousness that he was starting to form through his study of all of these alternative modalities, and he wanted to learn more.

So, in August of 1978, he enrolled in Monroe's 10-day program at the Monroe Institute. Monroe's theory revolved around the idea that out-of-body experiences (OBEs) were something anyone could learn to experience at will, not just be subjected to randomly or spontaneously. In his programs, he taught others the hands-on skills and methods he used to induce OBEs. The basic idea is that one can separate the consciousness from the physical body and travel anywhere they like, seeing, hearing, and experiencing different places as though they were physically there.

The CIA even employed the Monroe Institute in 1977 to train military operatives in a parapsychological intelligence connection technique they termed "remote viewing" with an intent of spying on Soviet operations. The project was called Gondola Wish. Monroe's methods—used by the CIA as well as everyday participants in his programs—include using binaural beat music, which can be found commonly all over the Internet and meditation tracks today.

During his 10 days of learning Monroe's method, David lay on his back in a comfortable, softly lit room, listening to binaural beats through large headphones. Along with the track, Monroe would lead a guided meditation with a calm and soothing tone of voice. While guiding the participant to relax all parts of their body and drift off to sleep, he would repeat the intention for them to have an out-of-body experience over and over. By June of 1979, the guided meditations were also available via a tape subscription service for members of the Monroe Institute. Soon, David found he could experience OBEs, which are also called astral projections, almost at will. David practiced at this a lot, becoming adept at traversing the astral realms. He liked to relate a humorous story in which once, when he came back into his body, he went in upside down on accident. He was looking at the back of his skull down at the floor, and had to back his astral form out of his body to "redock" properly.

He also later related of this form of exploration:

> I only had one such experience with spirit guides, I think. I went to the Monroe Institute and learned astral projection, and one time, in an altered state of consciousness—I think it was level 12 for those of you who have done the Monroe tapes—I was concerned with something about the future, so I'm intentioning a vision about something off in the distant future. All of a sudden, a voice in my head said, "Try living one day at a time." Brought me back to reality.[22]

This exploration, though seen as too far into the paranormal realm of things for many of his close staff and colleagues, only further confirmed David's ideas about the capabilities of the human mind and spurred his ongoing investigation into consciousness.

REBIRTHING

David was introduced to the idea of rebirthing in 1979 by a friend who was a rebirther—or instructor in rebirthing. This alternative therapy technique was developed in the 1970s by psychologist Leonard Orr to help people release emotions. The idea behind it is to investigate and fully let go of any trauma that may be associated with the experience of being born—a difficult and strange transition that all humans experience. By "rebirthing" oneself, a person can release stored stress and become more in tune with their inner world and feelings. It generally employs a breathing technique called conscious energy breathing, which includes cycles of rapid hyperventilation while the patient lies on their back for about 20 minutes. A qualified instructor should always be supervising.

There are many different types of this therapy now, but David experienced it in a group setting and found it quite freeing.

※ ※ ※

David was an avid explorer during this decade. Though he was always a skeptic and could not stop from engaging his critical and intellectual side, he prided himself on remaining open to trying anything that seemed like it held promise. He followed a rigorous set of standards for each new modality he encountered. First, he would fully immerse himself in it, reading all the available material and making sure he understood the theory behind it. Then, he'd find a way to experience it, whether through a course or other means. The practical experience always revealed the truth to David. Theory wasn't enough.

Not everything worked for David; for example, he wasn't able to get anything from transcendental meditation, a technique for silent meditation that is meant to induce inner calm and stillness along with access to higher consciousness. His quest led him to try out other modalities such as: bodywork like reiki and reflexology, treatments from alternative practitioners like chakra balancing, and different kinds of therapy.

It was a time of learning, unlearning, and taking everything in. David was a sponge, soaking up ideas from doctors, gurus, and everything in between as he charted a path toward his true purpose.

CHAPTER 8

WESTWARD AND INWARD

All the internal work that David had been doing throughout the 1970s opened up a new door inside him. Things that used to matter (or at least feel important due to social pressure), like prestige with his business and material wealth, just seemed unimportant. There was a new motivation inside him connected to his burgeoning ideas about the potential for human consciousness.

Things were bubbling up. His marriage, which had been steadily dissolving since the death of his daughter, was formally over in 1978. They had grown apart. Margaret didn't really understand his intense searching, and her own ideas did not align with the direction his spiritual understanding was evolving toward. By the summer of 1979, David was 52 years old, and he'd made his decision: he would end his career as a psychiatrist. He would leave his practice and all its offshoots. He would move away from New York.

This meant leaving behind his family, his social and professional connections, his multimillion-dollar home that he'd painstakingly designed and built, and even his esoteric library, which had swelled to over 6,000 volumes. But David had made his peace with that. He didn't need any of those things. He put his affairs in order, leaving the North Nassau Mental Health Center to longtime staff member Charlie Tkaz, who was a pediatric psychiatrist. Though the clinic continued applying David's methods, it struggled after he left. David was the beating heart of the place, and as he'd previously discovered, the consciousness of the doctor is extremely impactful on the outcome of the patients. The clinic eventually shuttered in 2000.

Randy Richmond, known to his friends as J. R., decided to accompany David on his journey. J. R. was a former alcoholic and patient of David's, and they had maintained a close friendship ever since he'd become sober through therapy and other supportive techniques at North Nassau. While David was deep-diving into the Human Potential Movement, J. R. was having a similar renaissance that included *A Course in Miracles* and Jungian studies. The pair—while opposites in many ways—never lacked topics for stimulating conversation. J. R. was quite unusual and quite the character, but he helped David to make positive changes in his life. He was always a good influence and a good friend.

Though this move seemed sudden to even David's close friends and colleagues, in a lot of ways, it had also been a long time coming. It was also a necessary move to truly untether himself from his old self and all the expectations and baggage that went along with that. David and J. R. packed what seemed important into his old, beat-up pickup truck and, on August 5, headed west without much of a plan other than their destination: Sedona, Arizona.

THE CATHEDRAL WITHOUT WALLS

Of course, David's interest in Sedona was initially piqued because of his successful experience with the Sedona Method. Levenson had settled on this name for the process he developed after moving away from the hustle and bustle of New York City to the quiet, contemplative little Arizona town, where the Sedona Training Institute remains to this day.

Nestled amid the breathtaking red rock landscapes of northern Arizona, Sedona stands as a beacon of natural beauty and spiritual allure. The town is renowned for its mesmerizing, otherworldly vistas. A part of what's known as the red rock region, Sedona's captivating, colorful sandstone formations erupt out of the landscape like standing stones created by the earth itself. Hiking through the area can feel like being on a different planet, with the red rocks in striking contrast against the stunning, blue sky.

Beyond its breathtaking geological features, Sedona has earned a reputation as a spiritual mecca, drawing seekers, healers, and those in search of higher consciousness. The region is adorned with vortex sites, believed by many to be natural centers of powerful energy conducive to meditation, self-reflection, and spiritual awakening. The most well-known vortices are Bell Rock, Boynton Canyon, Red Rock Crossing (also called Cathedral Rock), and Airport Mesa. Some people also consider Sedona to be a UFO hotbed.

Whether exploring the vibrant art scene, partaking in holistic wellness practices, or simply basking in the tranquility of its sacred landscapes, the Sedona of today beckons those seeking a deeper connection with nature and the spiritual realms. It is even called a "cathedral without walls," paying homage to the sacred, almost religious way that people—visitors and locals alike—feel about it. This harmonious blend of awe-inspiring scenery and metaphysical energy has positioned Sedona as a unique sanctuary for spiritual exploration and rejuvenation.

While now Sedona is widely known and celebrated as a unique spiritual place, at the time, it was only just becoming known, though the population was already on the rise, from 2,000 in 1970 to 5,300 in 1980. (As of 2024, it is home to about 10,000 full-time residents.) In just a few short years, the secret would be out, and Sedona would be considered America's new age capital. This was spurred in part by author Dick Sutphen's 1978 book, *Past Lives, Future Loves*, in which he described a psychic experience he had while visiting a Sedona vortex. But when David and J. R. arrived, it looked more like a small ranch town, ripped right from the pages of a Western novel. It was quiet and peaceful with a cowboy flavor. Ranches, horses, guns, and cowboy attire were the norm. The main downtown area consisted of one two-lane highway and two traffic lights. Beyond a small grocery store, a few restaurants that closed at 8 P.M. sharp, and a one-screen movie theater called the Flicker Shack, there wasn't much to see.

David traded his physician's garb for blue jeans, cowboy boots, and a wide-brimmed hat to block the relentless Arizona sun. He often wore plaid button-up shirts with vests, and though his hair had been a dark black-brown for much of his life, a distinguished gray started creeping in around this time, right on schedule for his upcoming time as a hermit.

Despite a fair amount of culture shock, he felt that this was where he was meant to be. Arizona, with its dry heat, seemingly infinite vistas, few people, and rugged terrain was a far cry from the concrete jungle he'd grown accustomed to in New York City. The desert was quiet, especially so at night when the darkness outside was absolute. Many residents in the area were people like David, those who'd had high-powered careers and were now called to the more peaceful lifestyle, those who were on a spiritual path and wanted a simpler life, or those simply looking for a beautiful place to retire. Everyone knew everyone else, and they all helped each other out. It was the kind of place where you didn't have to lock your doors at night.

The pair moved into an unfurnished house provided by an acquaintance of David's and became accustomed to a simpler, slower-paced kind of life. There was a collection of writers, artists, metaphysically inclined, and other eclectics who had been drawn to the area, and they would all gather at a local café—one of the only restaurants in town. David would eat there several times a week and got to know the crowd of regulars, quickly becoming one himself.

BECOMING THE HERMIT

David found himself turning inward, entering a reclusive state of contemplation and inner self-study, especially after J. R. found his own place and moved out. He busied his body with tasks like planting trees around the barren yard and a garden—something he enjoyed but hadn't been able to cultivate for himself since his childhood. He busied his mind with meditation and reading spiritual texts. He would often sit in meditation for hours on end, going late into the night or even overnight while foregoing food and drink. His body just didn't seem to require much sustenance, and he'd have to remind himself to eat a little something every now and again. After so many years of outward exploration and searching,

David was turning inward and beginning to synthesize his ideas. He likened this time to what ascetic Buddhist monks go through.

The outside world still pulled at David, though, and he had obligations in New York for the next four years, including four meetings a year for the board of directors of North Nassau Clinic. David did his best to juggle the external with his awakening higher consciousness. Since his experience in the snowbank in 1939, he'd been aware of what he later dubbed the Infinite Presence. It came to him in waves of realization, but it was beyond language, beyond time, and it defied all description or attempts to pin it down.

Across the major spiritual experiences of his life, David was touched by this Infinite Presence until "the personal 'I' became the instrument of the Infinite Presence and went about and did as it willed."[1] David didn't feel an attachment to his body and mind as his own anymore; he knew that consciousness went beyond that. His personal self had disappeared in 1965 when he had his awakening. Who he thought of as "David" no longer existed.

During this time, David was also determined to release any lower emotions that still lay heavy on his heart. He began a process of continually letting go, using the Sedona Method for 10 days. On one of these trips to New York, David was on the 11th day of letting go, dining alone at a restaurant called Rothmann's on Long Island when:

> The Presence suddenly intensified until every thing and every person, which had appeared as separate in ordinary perception, melted into a timeless universality and oneness. In the motionless Silence, it became obvious that there are no "events" or "things"

and that nothing actually "happens" because past, present, and future are merely artifacts of perception, as is the illusion of a separate "I" being subject to birth and death. As the limited, false self dissolved into the universal Self of its true origin, there was an ineffable sense of having returned home to a state of absolute peace and relief from all suffering. It is only the illusion of individuality that is the origin of all suffering. When one realizes that one is the universe, complete and at one with All That Is, forever without end, then no further suffering is possible.[2]

It was fitting, in a way, that this realization happened in the mundanity of a bustling New York restaurant rather than in solitude amid the spiritual landscape of Sedona. It was the snapping of David's last tether to his old self, his old beliefs, and his old consciousness that had begun in 1965 with the realization that caused his sobriety and kickstarted his enlightenment.

MEETING THE MASTERS

David was still very interested in seeking out variations on spiritual thought and attended many lectures from enlightened masters who would pass through the Sedona area. His interest wasn't in ascribing to any of these religions, and they didn't greatly influence his thoughts. But these kinds of masters also discussed enlightenment experiences similar to what David had gone through with the Infinite Presence. He investigated other spiritual teachings to confirm and better understand the high states and experiences that he was having. He started collecting books again and would eventually cultivate a massive spiritual library including many texts of

Eastern philosophy and religion. A few authors that especially influenced his thought were Huang Po, Ramana Maharshi, and Sri Nisargadatta Maharaj.

Huang Po was a Chan Buddhist master who lived during the Tang dynasty in China (circa 9th century). His teachings and writings, particularly compiled in *The Zen Teaching of Huang Po*, have had a profound influence on Zen Buddhism. Huang Po emphasized direct, experiential realization of one's true nature over intellectual understanding. His teachings often centered on the concept of "Mind" or "Buddha Mind," asserting that enlightenment is not something to be attained but a realization of one's inherent nature. He discouraged reliance on scriptures or rituals, encouraging a direct and immediate experience of enlightenment beyond conceptualization. Huang Po employed various skillful means, including shock tactics and paradoxical statements, to jolt students out of conceptual thinking and lead them to a direct, nondual understanding. His teachings laid the groundwork for the Rinzai school of Zen Buddhism, emphasizing the importance of direct experience and the ineffable nature of reality. Huang Po's profound insights into the nature of mind and his emphasis on direct experience continue to be studied and revered in Zen Buddhism today.

Ramana Maharshi, born in 1879 in South India, was a revered sage and one of the most influential spiritual figures of the 20th century. His teachings, often associated with Advaita Vedanta, emphasize self-inquiry and the quest for self-realization. Ramana advocated the practice of continuously asking the fundamental question "Who am I?" as a means to explore the nature of the self and discard the layers of ego and illusion. He emphasized the direct path to realization, bypassing complex rituals and intellectual pursuits. Ramana Maharshi's spiritual presence and teachings attracted a diverse array of seekers, ranging from the illiterate to scholars, all drawn to the transformative power of self-inquiry. His renowned works *Talks with Sri Ramana Maharshi* and the classic *Who Am I?* encapsulate his teachings, offering profound insights into the nature of consciousness and the path to inner awakening.

Sri Nisargadatta Maharaj was another 20th-century Indian spiritual teacher who unfolded profound insights into the nature of reality and self-realization. Born in 1897 in Mumbai, he led a humble life as a small-scale bidi merchant (a type of flavored, hand-rolled cigarette). Nisargadatta's teachings, encapsulated in the seminal work *I Am That*, revolve around the philosophy of Advaita Vedanta. Central to his message is the inquiry into the sense of "I am," encouraging seekers to meditate on their essential consciousness. Nisargadatta emphasized transcending identification with the body-mind complex to recognize the timeless, formless reality underlying all phenomena. His direct and uncompromising approach echoes the ancient wisdom of the sages, advocating the realization that one is not merely a person but the universal consciousness itself.

With the understanding that came from studying the teachings of these sages, David began to coalesce the teachings and uncover their true transformative impact. Many of the ideas of the masters were simple yet transcendent—easy to understand and yet difficult to master. Specifically, the idea of Advaita—which is often translated as "nonduality"—felt like coming home to David. Nonduality is a central tenet in various Buddhist traditions, including Zen, Mahayana, and Tibetan Buddhism, and it underscores the path toward enlightenment, emphasizing the unity of all existence beyond conventional distinctions.

"In duality," as David later wrote, "manifestation is perceived as linear, and therefore, there are both a cause and an effect to be conceptualized and perceived."[3] Simply put, then, nonduality means recognizing that reality lacks a separate and permanent existence. It's the idea that everything is interconnected, and there is no enduring, independent self. Buddhism teaches that this belief in a fixed self is an illusion causing suffering. Instead, it encourages shedding the illusion of an unchanging self, discovering that the very notion of "self" is as fluid as a flowing river. The boundary between "self" and "other" dissolves. The understanding of nonduality involves realizing the interdependence of all things and going beyond the conventional view of self and others. This insight is often achieved through meditation and a direct experience of impermanence and emptiness.

This concept was clearly highly influential to David, and he would even develop the term "devotional nonduality" later on. This would be defined as a spiritual approach that emphasizes surrender, love, and devotion as a means to transcend the ego and attain a direct connection with the divine. In his later teachings, this path involves letting go of the ego's attachments and surrendering to a higher power, acknowledging the unity that underlies all of existence. Devotional practices, such as prayer, are viewed as gateways to spiritual realization, allowing individuals to align their consciousness with higher states of being. David suggested that through unwavering devotion and the dissolution of personal desires, one can merge with the divine, experiencing a profound sense of oneness and love that goes beyond dualistic distinctions. Devotional nonduality, in David's framework, becomes a transformative journey of the heart, leading individuals toward the recognition of their inherent divinity and the interconnectedness of all life.

David also experienced a renewed interest in Christianity, the faith of his childhood that he'd left behind all those years ago. During his awakening, he'd had a realization that God, as expressed through Christianity, was the Eternal Presence. There was no separation, no place where God was not. He was reconciling his rejection of that dogma, which had solely been based on the idea that he couldn't square the idea of a wrathful, vengeful God. Now, he was realizing that the spiritual ideas embedded in religious belief went far beyond that.

> In contradistinction to the intellectual approach in religious education, what we are describing here is the inner path. It arises from within. A religious education can set the stage for it, but it does not cause it. One can study theology day in and day out, and that study will not necessarily precipitate an inner spiritual realization. However, if there is an interest in religion, plus a certain motivation, the inner path becomes activated. The great saints of Christianity demonstrate that scriptural study, worship, and the devotion to religion can end up as a mystical inner awareness.[4]

He found that, for him, spiritual texts from different religious understandings and backgrounds didn't negate each other. There was always something, some spark of wisdom or truth, that would radiate through the text and become apparent. More often than not, the religious texts echoed each other in beautiful and meaningful ways.

David would spend the next seven years in deep meditation and study, the seeds of this and other ideas germinating in the dark, getting ready to be revealed to the world.

CHAPTER 9

CHARTING THE MAP OF CONSCIOUSNESS®

Though this was a time of intense study and contemplation, David also began sharing what he'd learned about the Sedona Method, muscle testing, *A Course in Miracles*, and nonduality by giving a series of 12 lectures he recorded on tapes and offered free of charge to anyone who wanted to listen to them. These were created in the early 1980s titled "Twelve Visits with the Good Doctor" and "had to do with the application of our research on the nature of consciousness as it applied to various illnesses. So, each of those twelve tapes applied to a different thing, such as heart disease or depression, or anxiety."[1] These talks were later translated into the book *Healing and Recovery*, and are also still available to view as streaming videos or audio MP3 files. Lectures would become an important part of the rest of David's life.

David wasn't focused on any specific path at this time; he was simply exploring his options. He thought he might become a monk or perhaps a minister for the progressive Unity Church that aligned with the ideas presented in *A Course in*

Miracles. But nothing quite encompassed his eclectic tapestry of spiritual understanding, and he decided to set off on his own. Initially called the Institute of Applied Spiritual Studies, he soon changed the name to The Institute for Spiritual Research, Inc., and this organization was officially established as a nonprofit in Arizona in 1983. It is still a functioning part of David's legacy today.

Through his nonprofit and other connections, David started branching out his lectures, including a series in Mexico as well as an ACIM-focused event in Egypt, where he got to realize his dream of meditating all night among the Great Pyramids. David also experienced countless synchronicities and miraculous moments during this time, which he attributed to his complete trust in the Infinite Presence to provide whatever he needed.

One story David would tell that elaborates the everyday miraculousness of this kind of experience was when he was once traveling down Highway 89A going toward Cottonwood. This is the scenic, main highway that runs east and west, and in those days, it was just two lanes. As he was going down the road, another car suddenly appeared, coming straight at him at what must have been 70 miles an hour. It looked like they were trying to get around the traffic in their lane, but they'd misjudged how close David's car was. He said a quick prayer, as an accident appeared unavoidable, but in the next moment, the speeding car was on the side of the road, and David passed by without incident.

In the early '80s, David moved to a small cabin on three and a half acres of land. Near the famous Cathedral Rock, it included access to a tributary of Oak Creek as well as the adjacent woods, and David was thrilled. He named his new home Rattlebone Ranch. The road leading down to the ranch was the Upper Red Rock Loop Road, and at the time, it was a winding, rough, unpaved road. By the time a driver would get down the hill, they'd feel like their fillings were going to fall out of their teeth and their bones had just about been rattled out of their body—hence the name! David immediately began cultivating a vegetable garden, planting fruit trees, and building space for a menagerie of animals that would include, at various times, chickens, ducks, pigeons, sheep, llamas, rabbits, goats, dogs, and a friendly brown-and-white donkey named Moonbeam. He also designed and constructed a water wheel powered by the stream and would later add several more cabins. David would live on the ranch for the rest of his life.

As always, David was the main force behind designing and building his new space. He was always hands-on and knew his way around constructing. And even in working on his home, David had a chance to test the skills he'd been cultivating. While using a circular saw, he inadvertently cut through his left thumb. "At first, there was shock, but then in that shock, there was suddenly a chorus in my mind. It was as though I was surrounded by angelic forces that kept chanting to me as though I had forgotten it, 'You are not a body; you are totally free.'"[2] At the hospital, the thumb needed surgery to be amputated, and David instructed the surgeon to go ahead without any anesthetic. He began letting go.

> Although the body was there, I no longer experienced it. Instead, I went into a state of infinite and profound peace beyond all description; it was an infinite inner joy and happiness that cannot be described. I remember that, in my mind, I was looking at the thumb or representation of it on a different plane

and felt happy at its removal because it symbolized something I wished to be rid of. What could have been an excruciatingly painful experience was instead ecstatic, and there was an exquisite knowingness that was surrounded by infinite peace. I was infinitely protected by the love of the universe, by God, and by the radiance of Divinity.[3]

This presence could take over at any time. One day, while at the dentist's office, David was in the chair and the dentist said, "We've got to pause; he's going into that state." David practiced what he preached, and he was practicing it long before he began to share what he'd learned with the world.

A RETURN TO PSYCHIATRY

Though his main focus was on his study of consciousness, David liked to keep an eye on what was going on in the world of medicine. He also noticed that there was a need in his community for some of the services that he used to provide in New York, especially for recovering alcoholics, people getting over drug addiction, and older people in the last phase of their earthly lives. So, in 1986, he passed the Arizona psychiatry licensing exam at age 59 and started a part-time practice offering services in Prescott, Arizona, about an hour and 20 minutes from Sedona. He drove to nursing homes in the area as well as seeing patients in his Prescott office and in a small cabin he constructed at Rattlebone Ranch for the purpose.

He was determined to keep this side of his life small, but David was never able to say no to people in need. This work began pulling him back into the world at large. Soon, he got a call from the Mingus Mountain Residential Estate Center, a rehabilitation facility that housed teenage girls ages 12 to 17, many of whom had suffered childhood trauma or were sent there by court order. The center offered a therapeutic approach in its program, utilizing therapy horses to support mental well-being and teach the girls about healthy relationships and boundaries. Today, the center is now called the Mingus Mountain Youth Treatment Center and is still home to thriving therapeutic rehabilitation and educational programs.

At the time, there were over 50 full-time residents, but they didn't have a doctor. David took the job and began making the 30-mile trek to Mingus Mountain several times a week. The drive was up a steep mountain pass, and it could be hazardous, especially in snowy or icy conditions, but David rarely missed a day. One day as David was traveling up the tricky pass, the roads were slippery because of recent rain and snow. A car was coming in the other direction and both vehicles hit an icy patch, beginning to swerve just as they reached each other. But miraculously, they both swerved around each other and went on their separate ways without a scratch! Another time, David turned off the main road onto the dirt road that led to Mingus Mountain's entrance. As he made the blind turn, he came upon a deer in the middle of the road. He didn't have time to react, but the deer jumped up right over the truck, its hooves hitting the roof with a loud clattering as it hopped over.

No matter what, his trusty old pickup truck chugged along, and David relied on the Infinite Presence, knowing that there was a larger plan at work. He'd get where he needed to go, or help would arrive right when he needed it. And it always did.

ALLNESS VERSUS NOTHINGNESS

Several hours each day would be spent meditating in what David called his monastery of one. He removed himself so much from the outside world that he wasn't aware of current events or popular culture. Sometimes, he wasn't even aware of himself and would surprise himself in the mirror, thinking, *Who is that?* There was a core truth that David was trying to find, centering around the question of: What is the nature of absolute reality?

During this time, he was focused on letting go of all attachments, which meant negating his identification of his self, his body, his thoughts, and his emotions. His meditative sessions brought him to the brink of spiritual ecstasy; "it was like being in love with everyone," and David sometimes found it difficult to return to the material world after these blissful experiences.[4] Once during meditation, David reentered what he came to term the Void, which he had previously thought might be the ultimate state of enlightenment.

> The Void is seemingly complete and sufficient unto itself, as well as being impressive by virtue of its stillness and peace, along with the absence of ideation or any other form of linearity. "Surely," the devotee believes, "this is the state of Enlightenment," as the condition is still, peaceful, truly void, and not limited to time or space. The Void is also free of emotions or perceptions as it is nonlinear and thereby devoid of such options.[5]

David realized that what he'd been thinking was non-attachment was actually detachment, "an ongoing process that, unfortunately, can lead to apathy and emotional flatness, noninvolvement, and indifference."[6] The nothingness that this created was not aligned with the Infinite Presence he'd previously experienced. David later noted that this state was something he'd experienced in other lifetimes, and it was a state that he'd been stuck in.

> This final duality of whether the Ultimate Reality is existence or nonexistence had first presented itself in this lifetime at age three. This soul had gone that way before and, as a spiritual adept, had chosen the Void. Thus, at each physical death, consciousness went into the Void because of its belief in its reality, and then it was shocked and surprised to find itself back in another physicality. If the Void were the Ultimate Reality, no return to consciousness would have been possible.[7]

So, if not the Void, then what was Ultimate Reality? During this meditation session, David realized that "beyond Voidness is the ultimate, all-inclusive nonlinear reality of Allness."[8] And what was that Allness? It was love. But not just any love; it was Divine Love, a timeless quality that David had previously confused with "personal emotional love" and therefore tried to negate "as an attachment, emotionality, and specialness associated with dependence, and desire."[9] Now, he realized that Divine Love was something different. "Divine Love is predominant, powerful, overwhelming, and the primary quality or essence of the Presence. It is profound and unconditional, with no subject or object. It is not an emotionality but a condition or a state that is liberating rather than limiting."[10]

"Divine Love, like the sun, is unconditional," David would later write. "Limitation is a consequence of the ego."[11] Perhaps there is no simpler or more profound distillation of his work.

Alongside this discovery, there was a reopening of his heart and his understanding of the beauty of that other kind of love, the personal emotional love. And it was just in time: the person he'd been meant to find all along was on her way.

FOR THE LOVE OF DANCE

Anyone who knew David later in his life would say that he delighted in dance, but they might be surprised to find out that it wasn't always that way.

Through much of his life, he'd been nervous to the point of having anxiety attacks about speaking or performing in public, and even still, David tended to shy away from the limelight. His teachings and lectures were not large at this time, and though he delighted in one-on-one or small-group conversations, the idea of a crowd was too much for him.

He also had not considered himself a great dancer despite having to attend a plethora of debutante and cotillion parties for his daughters along with other formal and informal events during his years in Manhasset. He was awkward and self-conscious, greatly envying those who were able to let their inhibitions go and glide gracefully around the floor. Then, at one event in the early 1970s, his daughter Barbara dragged him onto the dance floor despite his protests. She told him to just stop looking at his feet, to just feel the music and do what she was doing.

He immediately sensed an ease come over his body—and he was dancing! There was nothing to it. After that, he became an avid, even insatiable dancer, and considered it a kind of ecstatic experience. "He surrendered to the dance, and then the dance was dancing him."[12] David was able to dance for hours on end, never tiring but only feeling extreme elation and energy. In Sedona, there was a vibrant country-western dancing scene, and David would venture out to take part. It was at a country-western dancing class at the Sedona Elks Lodge in 1988 that he met Susan Jane Humphrey.

Susan grew up on a small country farm in Iowa—their rural upbringings were something that she and David had in common. Her parents were Presbyterian and could be strict, yet they were also down-to-earth and instilled in her a strong work ethic and a love for growing things. The small-town life was restricting, though, and Susan longed to escape the judgmental, all-seeing eyes of the town. She moved with her family to Phoenix, Arizona, when she was 12 years old, and there she felt set free and filled with new ideas.

She put herself through school by modeling clothing and jewelry and later worked in boutiques and art galleries throughout Arizona. She always had an open interest in spirituality, especially ideas that went beyond what her Christian--based upbringing had offered. Despite years of attending church every week, she never felt a strong connection to those beliefs. She got married young, and her first marriage lasted 13 years, but they got divorced shortly after Susan got pregnant. She remarried quickly after that, feeling the stress of needing to support her new baby, a girl she named Sarah. But that marriage didn't work out either.

An avid dancer all her life, Susan adored going out dancing. As Susan recounts in her memoir, *Life with "Doc,"* at that country-western class, she and David "saw each other from across the dance floor, and it was an instant recognition. I was never one to believe in love-at-first-sight 'lightning bolts,' but that's what it felt like."[13] David asked Susan to be his dance partner that day, but neither of them knew it was going to be a partnership that would last for the rest of their lives! For now, though, they were happy to just dance the night away.

THE MAP COMES INTO BEING

David didn't reveal his spiritual side to Susan right away, but one day in 1989, about six months into their relationship, Susan was visiting David's home to have dinner. She noticed a chalkboard he had set up with a chart on it. Curious, she asked David what it was, and he introduced her to his Map of Consciousness®. This was something David had been working on for the last few years, and he had already been taking it out for test drives with some of the talks that he'd given in the early to mid-'80s. He felt it might be the culmination of his years of self-study—and the start of something new.

The Map of Consciousness® is a logarithmic scale of consciousness that came out of a composite of at least 20 years of research in a variety of fields. "On a single chart," David told Susan when she first encountered the Map, "you see the entire world. It's the level of consciousness that determines how a person sees the world. It shows the pits of despair all the way to the state of enlightenment."[14]

As David conceived of it, "the energy field of consciousness is infinite in dimension," by which he meant that time and space were meaningless when investigating the truth of the energy of anything.[15] As David wrote in his first book on the topic, *Power vs. Force*, "Data is useless until we know what it means. To understand its meaning, we need not only to ask the right question; we also need the appropriate instruments with which to measure the data in a meaningful process of sorting and description."[16]

On the Map (see page 165), one sees six columns that describe the general fields of consciousness. The arrows in the center of the chart show the direction of the field, with upward arrows indicating a positive direction and downward arrows indicating a negative one. There are six columns on the Map, and the best way to understand it is to begin in the middle, with the Level and Log columns.

Building on the emotional levels he learned from Virginia Lloyd and the scale created by Vern Black, David used kinesiology to calibrate numerical values for each of the 17 different levels of consciousness, ranging from the lowest to the highest:

Shame (20)
Guilt (30)
Apathy (50)
Grief (75)
Fear (100)
Desire (125)
Anger (150)
Pride (175)
Courage (200)
Neutrality (250)
Willingness (310)
Acceptance (350)
Reason (400)
Love (500)
Joy (540)
Peace (600)
Enlightenment (700–1,000)

"When we're talking about consciousness, we're talking about energy fields," David said in one of his recorded talks from the 1980s.[17] Higher energy fields correspond with higher numerical calibrations. The fields below Courage (200) convey a downward direction and are anti-life; they do not support life and are considered the Levels of Weakness (what David called "force"). The fields above Courage go in an upward direction, a positive direction. These support and nurture life and are the Levels of Truth (called "power"). The higher and more powerful the energy, the more aligned with Truth it is.

The other four columns of the Map share "key aspects in human experience that correlate to each level of consciousness:".[18]

- The God View, or how a person understands God from that level, which accounts for the wide range of theological beliefs.
- The Life View, or the perception that a person has of themselves at that level.
- The Emotions experienced within that level.
- The Process going on within consciousness itself at that level.

For example, 100 is the Level of "fear." The God View is "punitive," the Life View is "frightening," the Emotion felt is "anxiety," and the Process is "withdrawal."

Altogether, the Map provides a scale, known as the Hawkins Scale or the Scale of Consciousness, where individuals can locate their current emotional and mental states. "An individual's level of consciousness is determined by the principles they're committed to."[19] Embracing higher vibrational states leads to personal growth, well-being, and spiritual evolution.

Though it's presented linearly to help our logical minds categorize and comprehend it, it is not experienced that way. In the introduction to *The Map of Consciousness Explained*, David writes, "You don't go from one level to the next in linear fashion. It's more accurate to say it's phasic, like the weather."[20] Throughout life, everyone experiences the whole Map. By creating a visual representation of these universal experiences, David "wanted to reassure those who are suffering that there's something better ahead" and to "inspire them to become more loving and compassionate."[21]

> The purpose of the Map of Consciousness® is to create a context out of which merely experiencing it, merely seeing it, opens whole new avenues; whole new avenues begin to just open up automatically and our intention now is facilitated; our capacity to heal ourselves and to heal others, the fulfillment of our own potential as we see ourselves move forward in our own realization of the Truth.[22]

Susan was immediately struck by the life-changing potential of the Map of Consciousness®. She encouraged David to share it with others, telling him that it could really help people. David had been offering a lecture about once a month called "Calibrations of Levels of Consciousness: Spiritual Validity" to recovering addicts and alcoholics at Sedona Villa, and the response had already been positive, helping him further refine his ideas. But perhaps Susan's encouragement was what he really needed to get the ball rolling. Soon after, she became his right arm—literally! Muscle testing became David's main technique for deciphering what level of consciousness something was, or, as he called it, consciousness calibrating.

The muscle-testing response is a simple "yes" or "not yes" (no) response to a specific stimulus. It is usually done by the subject holding out an extended arm and the tester pressing down on the wrist of the extended arm, using two fingers and light pressure. Usually the subject holds a substance to be tested over their solar plexus with the other hand. The tester says to the test subject, "Resist," and if the substance being tested is beneficial to the subject, the arm will be strong. If it is not beneficial or it has an adverse effect, the arm will go weak. The response is very quick and brief.[23]

Initially, it was believed that the response was due to the nervous or immune system of the body. But later research would find that it was

> a general response of consciousness itself to the energy of a substance or a statement. That which is true, beneficial, or pro-life gives a positive response that stems from the impersonal field of consciousness, which is present in everyone living. This positive response is indicated by the body's musculature going strong. There is also an associated pupillary response (the eyes dilate with falsity and constrict to truth) as well as alterations in brain function as revealed by magnetic imaging.[24]

This testing could be done on any part of the body, but for convenience, David generally had his subject hold out their arm and use their deltoid muscle.

Susan became David's consciousness calibration partner. She would hold out her arm for David to test all kinds of different truths, even hundreds during single sessions when he was working on writing *Truth vs. Falsehood*. Through muscle testing, they also discovered that they'd been together for 11 previous lifetimes—it was no wonder they'd found each other in this one and felt an immediate knowing about each other.

CHAPTER 10

THE WORK BEGINS

Not long after his experience of awakening and discovery of the truth of Divine Love, David found himself faced with another spiritual trial around 1987. His state of consciousness, stirred by the work he was doing, started to evolve again and progress. Remembering the strain that he'd gone through to relearn how to be in the world after his first raising in consciousness, David felt an initial trepidation, but he easily let it go, knowing that there was a higher plan for him. During this time, he found himself subject to psychic attacks by what he termed "demons" that "represented the collective energies of the lower ego states that had accumulated in consciousness over great expanses of time."[1]

On one occasion, something even more momentous happened, which David referred to as the "high-altitude fail/pass test": "There was no worldly presence, but on the consciousness level, there was an encounter with a more rarified Luciferic presence that promised great power if one went into agreement with it."[2] David later wrote that the being very subtly conveyed the following to him:

> Now that you are released from the attachment of love and realize that all karma was only based on illusion and that there is no fearsome, judgmental God or any "others" to be encountered, and now that you are beyond form and therefore beyond karma and totally free, your power is unlimited. Own that power as yours.[3]

After he refused, the being retreated, and he no longer experienced psychic attacks. This experience happened spontaneously—something that David would stress anytime he spoke of or wrote about it. In Susan's words, "Dave said it's not something that you yourself can 'make happen.' It's what you have *become* as a consequence of Divine Will and Divine Grace. It occurs of its own when the time is right, and it has nothing to do with *you*."[4]

Of the moment, David later wrote that he "could see and know that Christ had passed through that temptation and had also refused it."[5] Though difficult to fully contemplate—or even for David to put into words—this moment represented his ascent to true enlightenment. This was a state that David never claimed for himself, though many others would call him an enlightened being throughout the years. David only referred to it as transcending the levels of consciousness, which always came with a paradox of dualities that had to be solved.

After this experience, David never sat in formal meditation again. He did still often do what he simply called contemplation. This is more of a continual being with the self and with higher consciousness that can be done anywhere and anytime—it doesn't require the focused discipline and container of meditation.

WRITING THE WORK

At first, David wasn't sure about sharing the Map of Consciousness® with the wider public. He had been in Sedona for a decade and enjoyed his quiet, contemplative existence. He was already seeing the power of the Map in himself and for others through just his small Sedona Village lectures and knew even more people could benefit.

With the help of the Map and the variety of modalities he experimented with, David was even able to cure himself of medical issues that had been plaguing him. As David later recalled:

> I went to see an internist and he said, "Well, you've got COPD [chronic obstructive pulmonary disease] and heart failure, there is nothing we can do about it." So, I went home to die. And I had a cutting edema, it's called anasarca. It's so severe that your whole body swells up and when it gets to the heart, you croak, so I figured, well. I put the house in order. Made sure things were neat and sweet and orderly and ready to go. . . .
>
> And I just kept going as long as possible—when the cops stopped me and he said I could not drive and said, "You better go see your doctor." So anyway, I went to an emergency room in Cottonwood and a wonderful doctor, an internist who's been my internist ever since looked at me and he said, "That's the worst case of Graves' disease I've ever seen."[6]

David had been misdiagnosed by the original internist, and though they wanted to take the thyroid out surgically,

David said, "Well, I don't think I want to do that. No, I have my own ways of doing things."

Along with Susan's urging that the work could be beneficial to many, David felt the pull to write a book. But he also knew, in the back of his mind, that a book would be the end of his monk-like solitude.

He began the writing process in 1990 while juggling his ranch duties, weekly sessions with patients in Sedona and Prescott, and the physician's job at Mingus Mountain. He somehow found time on top of all of that to devote to his garden and tinker with his inventions—a lifelong hobby of his. David always knew how to keep busy, but even all that wasn't enough. He decided to get his Doctor of Philosophy degree. After a bit of research, he discovered that he could enroll at Columbia Pacific University via a distance-learning program and study at his own pace without ever leaving home. David signed up right away in March of 1991 and by the end of September 1995, he was awarded a Ph.D.

While still working on his dissertation—which was titled "Qualitative and Quantitative Calibration of the Levels of Human Consciousness"—he felt that his manuscript, which he had titled *Power vs. Force*, was complete. This book broke down the Map of Consciousness®, detailing how David had created it and what each of the levels meant. He intended it to be read for personal development, so readers could cultivate a more conscious and fulfilling life.

David began looking for a publisher. He had no idea how the publishing process worked, but through a connection in New York, he got the manuscript to an industry professional. They gave the material a lukewarm review, telling David that he wasn't going to get it published by a major house; it just wasn't the kind of material they were interested in.

The Work Begins

No matter. Now that the book was complete, David was determined to put it out in the world. He knew, just like at every other crossroads in his life, that the right opportunity would come along at the right time. While polishing the manuscript, David had worked with an editor who gave him the idea of self-publishing. This appealed to David, because it meant that he would have full control over the book's appearance and final contents, not something that he would find at any publishing house.

Taking out a second mortgage on his ranch and home, he created Veritas Publishing, which to this day is the exclusive owner and purveyor of Dr. Hawkins's books and video and audio lectures, existing wholly to provide his work to the world. David chose the word *veritas* because it means "truth" in Latin, and that's just what he planned to offer the world with his work.

Power vs. Force was published by Veritas in 1994. It had an initially quiet reception, which was to be expected from a self-published venture. David had no interest in marketing or self-promotion, and "lived by the principle of 'attraction not promotion,'" as Susan said.[7] He believed wholeheartedly that the book would find the audience it was meant to find. The books were kept in boxes in one of the cabins on his property, and they would ship out the orders themselves. In the first year it sold about 300 copies, which was more than David expected. But more important than how many copies were being sold was what people thought. It was favorably reviewed in smaller publications, and slowly but surely, seekers who were looking for the truths that David had discovered started finding the book.

By the time *Power vs. Force* was published, David had been researching and tinkering with the Map of Consciousness®

over "a twenty-year period, involving millions of calibrations on thousands of test subjects of all ages and personality types, and from all walks of life."[8]

> Contemplation of the Map of Consciousness® can, for instance, transform one's understanding of causality. As perception itself evolves with one's level of consciousness, it becomes apparent that what the world calls the domain of causes is in fact the domain of effects. By taking responsibility for the consequences of their own perceptions, observers can transcend the role of victim to an understanding that "nothing out there has power over you." It is not life's events, but how one reacts to them and the attitude that one has about them, which determine whether the events have a positive or negative effect on one's life, whether they are experienced as opportunity or as stress.[9]

The Map would be the cornerstone of his work for the rest of his life, the apex of his contribution to the world, and the ultimate way in which he would be able to help the most people he possibly could.

But the work was only just beginning.

PART FOUR

THE FINAL DOORWAY
1999–2012

CHAPTER 11

THE WORK MEETS THE WORLD

Initially, Susan and David had planned to get married in 1991, but it fell through at the last minute. Sarah was only 10 years old at the time, and Susan decided she needed to make her daughter her number-one priority while she was still growing up. But despite that first try not working out, David and Susan continued to be drawn together, and by 1997, she'd moved into Rattlebone Ranch. On December 26, 1999, they were finally wed in a small, private ceremony on the ranch. The third time was the charm—for both of them.

In coming out of his monastery for one, David realized there was a lot in the world that he needed to catch up on. He began reading the newspaper religiously and watching the news to gain a closer understanding of all kinds of world events. This would begin to be even more important as he began writing more.

THE MAP TAKES FLIGHT

Susan's prediction was correct: slowly but surely, the Map started gaining attention. Many people were finding it extremely useful and life-changing—and they wanted more. In 1997, the book was translated into Korean—the book would go on to be published in 25 languages—and little did they know, but it was making big waves there. Both *Power vs. Force* and David's next book, *The Eye of the I* (which would be published in 2001), would become bestsellers in South Korea. Despite the books finding their audience and continuing to sell well, that was never the case in the United States. Susan and David were delighted when they were contacted by a group of people from South Korea who wanted David to come and lecture there.

The pair ended up traveling to South Korea in 1999 and 2000. This kind of international travel was a very different, exciting, and slightly intimidating situation that neither of them had ever experienced before. Since they didn't know quite what to expect, they'd overpacked, bringing at least five pieces of luggage—each! So it was a challenge simply to get around with all their stuff. When they finally reached the airport in South Korea, there was no one there to meet them. They later found out that their guides had accidentally gone to the other airport. There were military guards with intimidating guns all over the airport, and the pair had a difficult time getting through customs even with their letter from the Buddhist teacher who was hosting them.

Finally out of the airport and into a taxi, they found communication difficult with a driver who only spoke Korean, of which they barely knew a word. They ended up at the wrong hotel—one that was way out in the woods—and after much confusion, the driver realized that the name of the hotel was misspelled on their reservation. They got to the right place in the end!

Part of the original contingent that came to persuade David to visit South Korea was Dr. Moon, a Buddhist teacher who had studied under the Dalai Lama and now headed her own ashram, or monastic community, in South Korea. David spoke at a college that Dr. Moon was affiliated with, and both he and Susan were flummoxed by the Korean custom where everyone would take off their shoes before entering the lecture area. The crowd that day was quite large, so outside the door was a huge mass of shoes! They worried they wouldn't be able to find their shoes after the lecture, but with some student help and by the grace of God, they did appear. Dr. Moon would become a close friend for the rest of David's life, often bringing her students to Sedona when he was hosting lectures. During their second trip to South Korea, David was awarded the title of Tae Ryoung Sun Kak Tosa, which meant Teacher of Enlightenment. The Korean people were very gracious and thankful, and David always appreciated their eagerness for his teachings. Dr. Moon's ashram created a huge feast displaying all their favorite Korean dishes for David and Susan, and they had quite the time sampling all the authentic Korean cuisine.

In fact, it was during David's second trip to South Korea that the inkling of the idea for *The Eye of the I* came to him. While his first book had mostly been an introduction and breakdown of what the Map of Consciousness® was, how it came to be, and the divide between the higher and lower levels, the piece that was missing was how a reader might begin to reevaluate themselves and begin the process of elevating their own awareness. *The Eye of the I* was to be a more instructive book.

In 2001, Wayne Dyer was given a copy of *Power vs. Force* by one of his students. Dyer was a guidance counselor and then a clinical psychologist before he wrote *Your Erroneous Zones*, which was published in 1976 and became an instant bestseller. It launched his career as an influential author and motivational speaker, and by 2001, he had already written over a dozen books. Focusing on the ideas of practical psychology and self-improvement, his main message was about helping people become their highest self and manifest their true desire.

He felt an instant connection with *Power vs. Force*. Dyer was so impressed that he got in touch with David. As Susan remembers it, Dyer called them on the phone and told David that he should consider having his book republished by Hay House, the publishing house where Dyer was an author. Hay House was an independent, spiritually focused publisher, and Dyer knew that through them, David's book and his incredible ideas could reach a wider audience. (Hay House remained independent until late 2023, when it was acquired by Penguin Random House.) Dyer had even spoken to his team at the publisher and shared the book with them; Hay House was interested.

David had no idea who Wayne Dyer was. He initially told him, "No, thanks" and thought that would be that. But Susan thought it wouldn't hurt to test the idea of making a connection with the publisher. "When we tested the question with kinesiology, the arm said it was for the highest good to sign a contract with Hay House."[1] In an unusual agreement, David negotiated the right to continue publishing the book through Veritas Publishing while giving Hay House the rights to publish their own version. At the same time, Dyer discussed *Power vs. Force* in his lectures, which reached hundreds of thousands of people around the globe. He even sold copies of the book on his lecture circuit. David's work was about to hit the mainstream.

THE LECTURES BEGIN

After the success of their lectures in South Korea, Susan brought up the idea of creating a lecture series in Sedona, something more formal and ongoing than the one-offs David had previously done. David was finally ready to accept the mantle of "teacher," something he had resisted despite the lecturing he'd previously done. It felt like a big deal to announce himself as a spiritual teacher, especially as he revered so many of the teachers that he'd been lucky enough to come into contact with. If he was going to call himself a teacher, he felt his offerings should reach a similar level of enlightenment. "As a doctor," he told Susan, "I can only help one person at a time. But if I go out and teach, I can help multitudes."[2]

That didn't mean he was giving up the mantle of "doctor," however. Though Susan knew David as "David," and always called him as such, those attending his lectures and his students knew him as "Doc" or "Dr. Hawkins," out of respect and devotion. (From this point on, Doc or Dr. Hawkins will be used to refer to David.)

They decided to host one all-day lecture each month in 2002 at Sedona's Creative Life Center. Dr. Hawkins's talks were always accompanied by pre-prepared lecture slides and often a whiteboard where he could write out or draw diagrams of concepts. He always started his lectures at the beginning, with a summary of the Map of Consciousness® and how calibration worked, whether or not there were new people in the audience. Dr. Hawkins believed in the value of hearing something over and over; that's how one really learned something. As he said, "Just hearing certain information is transformative."

By the time the lectures started in January of 2002, Doc's hair and beard had taken on a grayish-silvery hue. His face was lined, probably from his years of working in the Arizona outdoors. And, although he was small of stature, with his deep blue eyes, quick wit, and easy manner, Dr. Hawkins's presence commanded the stage. The January lecture had about 50 people in attendance, but that had already doubled by February. Dr. Hawkins wanted to provide lunch at the lectures, so Susan and another friend would take their pickup truck to Costco—which was an hour away—to load up on increasing amounts of food and drink for the participants. Each of these lectures and the lunches were provided free of charge to all attendees.

Throughout the lectures, Doc would walk back and forth across the stage, often stopping to point to his slides or look out at the audience. He had a familiar, accessible style that, along with imparting wisdom, included telling lots of jokes and personal stories. Dr. Hawkins loved to get the audience laughing, and he would always join in with his characteristic chuckle. His warm, resonating voice was captivating and clear, echoing easily throughout the room while attendees listened raptly. Susan was always sitting on the stage with him, sometimes helping out with calibrations or reminding Dr. Hawkins of certain facts when he wandered off course, as he inevitably did, to the delight of the listeners. By April, the space was filled to the brim with eager participants, and they had to start turning people away.

Toward the end of the year, Doc felt that the continued interest was so large and enthusiastic that he wanted to continue the monthly lectures, though they'd need to find a bigger venue. In the second year, the lectures were held at a nearby hotel, and there was so much interest, they had to institute a registration system. What was meant to be only 12 months would go on for the next 10 years. Susan also had the foresight to record every single one of these lectures, and they are still available through Veritas Publishing's streaming services.

In 2002, Dr. Hawkins was also working on the third installment in his book series, which would be titled *I: Subjectivity and Reality* and would be published in 2003. The book *I* delves deeper into metaphysical and philosophical concepts, expanding on the foundation laid by the first two books. These books formed a tight trilogy, and for a little while, Dr. Hawkins thought he was finished writing. But writing wasn't finished with him.

In the meantime, though, he was plenty busy. In 2003 and 2004, he gave six lectures in Sedona (one every other month), and during the alternate months, he and Susan were traveling to different areas in the United States and Canada. The outside talks were later called the "On the Road" series. Sometimes, just before a lecture, Doc would say, "I don't think I can give this lecture. I don't know what I'm going to say." Susan would need to reassure him that his higher self would come through. The minute he walked onstage, he would be fine, but it always scared the staff when he said this.

This time of the work was very exciting, and while many new people were getting the chance to be exposed to his ideas, devoted students would attend as many lectures as they could. Wherever Doc lectured, for the rest of his life, students would follow.

He also continued traveling abroad. Once, when giving a lecture at Oxford University in England, two students from India came up and bowed at his feet, kissing them and honoring him as their teacher. This was a very reverent moment, surprising to everyone there, especially Dr. Hawkins. It was the first time anyone did that. While traveling to offer lectures in Europe, Dr. Hawkins decided to visit as many cathedrals as he could, calibrating them along the way.

> My interest in Europe is the cathedrals because it is the greatest creative work of man. It combines the incredible architecture, incredible beauty, incredible commitment and work, incredible frescos, and paintings, carvings. You can look at a carving that a man has spent his entire lifetime carving—that pulpit. Everything in third and fourth dimension, and magnificent. And then of course, the incense over the couple of hundred years embeds itself in the wood. And then of course, you have the pageantry of the parade of the bishop and the miter and the incense. . . . You might say it reinforces a love of beauty, and one part of spiritual practice, I think, is an increasing sensitivity to beauty. And certainly, by the time you get to the high 500s, the beauty is stunning. In fact, it is incapacitating. As you get up around 580 or 590, the stunning beauty of the world makes you cry all the time. You can turn a corner and the beauty of it just knocks you out and you're really not too functional in the world.[3]

Based on this, he felt called to a new—and very ambitious—project: documenting and calibrating the breadth of human knowledge and experience. He and Susan would go on to do over 7,000 calibrations for this book, which would be titled *Truth vs. Falsehood* and published in 2005.

The calibrations discussed in the book include that of movies, music, spiritual teachers, sports and hobbies, classics of philosophy and literature, the animal kingdom (from the lowliest bacteria—1—to a dog's wagging tail—500),[4] and much more, including even the chapters and sections of the book itself. Dr. Hawkins said that the book was "the result of a lifetime dedicated to discovering the core and essence of Truth itself and how it can be recognized, expressed, and defined."[5]

LIVING WITH ENLIGHTENMENT

Even as there began to be more and more traction around the work, and there were endless opportunities for travel and lecturing, Doc was happiest when he could just live his humble, steady, quiet lifestyle. He told Susan, "All a person really needs is to feel loved and cared for, and I certainly have that!"[6]

Dr. Hawkins thrived in the outdoors and found gardening meditative. He was happiest when he could delight in nature, and he revered even the smallest moment. Nature gave him a sense of peace. The garden of vegetables and fruit trees that he'd planted upon moving in at Rattlebone Ranch had become a veritable Edenic landscape, and more often than not, Dr. Hawkins could be found out there tending to it, always accompanied by his menagerie of animals.

The area around Rattlebone Ranch was sometimes referred to by locals as Skunk Alley, because, for whatever reason, it was the perfect habitat for skunks and they simply thrived there. Of course, this could present a problem when they got too close to the house. Dr. Hawkins was often able to quietly catch a skunk without getting sprayed, after which he would put it in a skunk cage of his own devising, drive it a ways down the road, and let it go. This was one of his frequent tasks while living at Rattlebone Ranch. One time, Dr. Hawkins and Susan had just taken a skunk off the truck and carried the cage away from the road to let it go. A car came by and honked their horn, which spooked the skunk. It sprayed Dr. Hawkins and Susan before running off into the woods!

Animals, both domestic and wild, always had a large space in Doc's heart. One of his great joys was being able to raise a variety of animals, just like he'd done in his childhood. At one point, the Hawkinses were caring for "three cats, thirty chickens, several ducks, and a high-maintenance African Grey parrot," and yet Dr. Hawkins felt called to adopt a dog.[7] That was how Kelsey, a Border collie–Australian shepherd mix, came into their lives in early 2008. Susan had said, "I don't want a black dog," because she knew how their hair was much more visible—and how it would get all over the house! But of course, they ended up with a black-and-white, long-haired dog. When they went to the pound, "amongst all these howling dogs, there was one that just sat there. . . . It just glowed with a certain radiance."[8] After arm-testing right there in the pound, they knew Kelsey was coming home with them—and she tested at 255.

During their research for *Truth vs. Falsehood*, Doc and Susan had determined that pet animals have a large capacity for love and "exhibit an advanced development of the 'heart chakra' and have a therapeutic healing effect on people with a variety of illnesses."[9] This was definitely true of Kelsey, a steadfast girl with a warm and friendly disposition. She could always be found curled at Dr. Hawkins's feet and never missed a day of helping him collect the eggs from the henhouse.

A DECADE OF WRITING

As well as his writing and giving lectures, Dr. Hawkins was also doing talk show and phone interviews—the list is almost endless, but includes appearances with Oprah as well as *Good Day Arizona*, *The Larry James Show*, *Out of the Ordinary*, *Health Talk Radio*, *The Art Bell Show*, and many others. He also did a series of audio talk programs with Nightingale-Conant and recorded the audiobook of *Power vs. Force* himself.

In the new millennium, Dr. Hawkins was continually working on a writing project—usually more than one at a time—many of which were inspired by Susan. She seemed to be his muse, quietly giving him the energy and spark he needed to get his work out of his mind and down on paper. Dr. Hawkins mainly wrote in the third person, even when telling personal stories in his books. This set Dr. Hawkins the person at a remove from the content itself, which he saw simply as observation of the truths of the higher planes of consciousness that he'd been witness to. That distinction was important to Doc; he never wanted to be confused as some sort of oracle or put up on a pedestal. He simply wanted to share the truth.

As far as the process of writing went, while Dr. Hawkins would sit down to write during dedicated times, more often than not, he couldn't control when the insights would spontaneously arise in him. It often happened in the middle of the night, and he would reach for the white, lined notebooks that he kept close at hand wherever he went. Dr. Hawkins wrote everything longhand and never bothered to learn how to use a typewriter or a computer when those came along. He would also take dictation into a handheld cassette recorder, a practice preserved from his days as a physician, when this process was the norm for relaying patient histories and updates.

The first people to know about his in-progress works—besides Susan, of course—were the students attending his lectures. The talk series for each year would include material from whatever book he was writing at the time.

His fifth and sixth books, *Transcending the Levels of Consciousness* and *Discovery of the Presence of God*, were both published in 2006.

Transcending the Levels of Consciousness was Susan's idea. She thought it would be good to offer a more instructional book; instead of just explaining the theory and calibrations, why not give readers a manual for how to navigate the levels of consciousness for themselves? The book was "a practical manual rather than a comprehensive analysis," and it offered readers a chance to unpack the experiential blocks that were in the way of spiritual advancement.[10] Dr. Hawkins also updated his instructions for calibration with muscle testing.

Dr. Hawkins considered *Discovery of the Presence of God* to be his culminative text on understanding how to access spiritual truth. In it, he introduced the term "devotional nonduality," which signified the connection between the divine and the path of nonduality. He brought together the Western Christian devotion with the Eastern nonduality of no mind. To him, it meant a wholehearted commitment to the love of and search for truth. There are periods on the spiritual path that can be hard and arduous, and in those times, it takes the devotion from the heart and the love for God to keep going. The book, then, offered that "the pathway of Devotional Nonduality is a direct course to Enlightenment via clarification of core essentials that merely await activation by decision, intention, and dedication of the will."[11] At the beginning and ending of Doc's books can be found the phrase "Gloria in Excelsis Deo!" which comes from a Latin hymn and means "Glory to God in the Highest." It was also a phrase that he often said, and to him it was an exclamation of joy and pure love at the highest level. While he discusses God in his books, he considered them to be more spiritual than overtly religious, and "even though he wasn't defined by religion, he appreciated the sacredness of these rituals."[12]

His seventh book was *Reality, Spirituality, and Modern Man*, which came out in 2008. This book addressed the ills of modern society and the breakdown that Dr. Hawkins saw as caused by a lack of understanding about the true state of reality as beyond the world and our physical forms. The search for truth is something that humans at large have been after since the beginning of time, but mostly we haven't known how to go about it or test that the truths we were finding were reality. "The inability to discern actual truth from illusion is the primary obstacle of humanity overall and accounts for the vast majority of human problems as well as war and personal and social suffering."[13] The book took on the scope of history as Dr. Hawkins attempted to "clarify the difference between appearance/perception/illusion versus Reality/Truth/Essence."[14]

Now 80 years old, Doc was showing no signs of stopping, though he was no longer traveling outside of Arizona. In 2008, he gave some lectures at Yavapai College in Prescott, the high school in Prescott, as well as in Sedona. Though at this time, Doc was extremely busy with lectures, he had the idea to share some of the lectures he'd already done so they could reach a wider audience. With the help of his editor, he created a set of transcripts based on his "Twelve Visits with the Good Doctor" talks from the '80s about his understanding of illness and how to recover from it. These transcripts would become his eighth book, *Healing and Recovery*, which came out in 2009. "All illnesses are physical, mental, and spiritual, and the highest levels of recovery are the consequence of simultaneously addressing all three levels and seeing them as being of equal importance."[15]

Though he continued to take notes and write throughout the next four years, no more books would be published until after his death.

THE PATHWAY OF THE HEART

For almost the rest of his life, Dr. Hawkins would be constantly traveling and lecturing. It was a physically and mentally demanding lifestyle—and he hadn't even started teaching until he was in his early 70s!

Along with extensive lecturing across the United States, Doc and Susan lectured in Canada, England, and South Korea. They also traveled to Scotland, Ireland, and France. He also spent time doing radio and television appearances. His appearances were often booked over two years in advance and almost always sold out.

During the three decades that Dr. Hawkins had lived in Sedona, it had grown and become world-renowned as a hotbed for spiritual seekers. While still relatively small, it was no longer the cow town with one restaurant! Due to this, there was a large influx of people willing to learn from him.

So, based on the Buddhist teaching format called the satsang, which meant "sacred gathering," Dr. Hawkins hosted question-and-answer sessions rather than just his pre-planned lectures. This allowed for more of a free-flowing conversation, and the spontaneity of it appealed to him. In these sessions, which ran from 2006 to 2011, they could really get at the truth of the moment.

While Doc was continually on the move for consciousness research, he still had to rely on his physical body to get him around, and he wasn't getting any younger. In 2005, he suffered the collapse of a thoracic vertebra while out working in his yard at home. Dr. Hawkins did not want to have the surgery recommended by his doctor, and dealt with the pain through acupuncture. Later, he discovered that he had extreme osteoporosis, which had contributed to this and other skeletal issues he'd experienced over the years, including eye problems that started in 2005 when Doc and Susan went on a cruise in Alaska.

Breaking your back is never a good thing, but it did cause Susan and Doc to realize that they were overdoing it. So many requests came in from all over the world, and Dr. Hawkins had a hard time saying no to people who wanted his help. But if he wanted to be around for long enough to share his message widely, he needed to slow down.

Around 2008, he was also beginning to struggle with macular degeneration, mostly due to not wearing sunglasses in the severe Arizona sunshine for over three decades. He had to give up driving, which had always been a source of comfort and a time for contemplation for him. His health restrictions led to a decrease in traveling for the rest of his life. Instead, they began to focus on other ways to share the Map of Consciousness® and his research in muscle testing, which included video and audio lectures. He was often interviewed by radio hosts, which was another way a lot of people found his work. Dr. Hawkins also spent a lot of time reading and responding to written correspondence, which, with the advent of e-mail, came in overwhelming amounts.

CHAPTER 12

THE HOME STRETCH

Doc's last—and largest—lecture took place in September of 2011 at a venue in Prescott, Arizona, to over 1,700 people who came to hear him speak in person. It was simply titled "Love." Dr. Hawkins sat for the duration, dialoguing with Susan on the lessons he wanted to share along with sharing pre-recorded segments. He spoke slower, but still with as much striking clarity as he always had. "Love empowers us," he said. "Forgiveness and love are transformative."[1] Though the session was less outwardly energetic, the room was filled with a vibrance of love, good humor, and many tears, always punctuated by his infectious laugh.

During the six-hour session, participants—some of whom had traveled from faraway countries such as Thailand, Australia, and South Africa—were given space to speak about what Doc's work had meant to them. The lecture finished with a bagpipe salute, and it was the culmination of his public life.

If Dr. Hawkins had one overarching message for his life's work, it was love. "Once you become loving, there are certain things you can never do again. But you can also perform the miraculous without labeling it miraculous. You can do things other people cannot do, and people will do things for you that they will not do for others. So, love has a very powerful, transformative effect."[2]

THE LAST YEAR

Away from the public eye for good this time, Dr. Hawkins knew that he was only going to be around for a little while longer. But that didn't mean the work was done with him. He spent a lot of the last year at home finishing up the manuscript for *Letting Go*. This was a project that Dr. Hawkins had begun in the 1990s, but he'd lent it to someone and never got it back. In a miraculous turn of events, someone contacted Dr. Hawkins and said they had found this manuscript, and would he like to have it back? Since it landed back in his life, Susan encouraged him to finalize it despite the fact that over 20 years had passed since he'd started it. Together, they also video-recorded eight fireside interactive dialogues on key topics of his work, called The Discussion Talks.

With Doc's instruction, Susan also put all his affairs in order, including how he wanted the publishing business and the foundation to be run. He wasn't afraid of death. It was something he'd long ago made his peace with, both through his experiences with others in their last moments and his explorations in higher consciousness. Dr. Hawkins believed it was something to have a lot of compassion around, first for others and then for ourselves. "When we look at the dying experience, we see that it is a surrendering and letting go. It is a willingness to open our hearts to be love to others. If we are contemplating dying, and if we are doing the things I have talked about, in the morning when we get up, we say to God, 'To those who are dying, I send my consciousness, I send my love and my willingness to be one with them.'"[3]

THE END AND THE BEGINNING

Doc's health, always complicated throughout his life, began to fail him. He had a stroke on the evening of August 11, 2012. Standing by the fridge, Susan watched as he suddenly slumped to the ground. Once she'd gotten him in a chair, she called two friends before phoning 911 and getting Dr. Hawkins to the nearest emergency room. He had another stroke at the hospital that night. Dr. Hawkins needed an MRI, but the local hospital didn't have a machine for that. He was airlifted to Phoenix, and while it seemed fairly obvious that he'd had a stroke—his left side was semi-paralyzed—the tests were inconclusive.

He spent the last weeks of his life in a hospital bed in the living room of their home at Rattlebone Ranch. Dr. Hawkins wanted to die at home, but he was determined to stay in his body for as long as possible, to pass on every piece of wisdom and every ounce of compassion and love. He signed case after case of books for future students. He even took time to talk through mundane little details, like e-mail correspondence. He knew that life would go on, and his work would go on, long past his earthly end. Dr. Hawkins had long believed that we don't really disappear when we die; we are just transformed to another state of being.

His spirits remained high, and his humor was just as warm and infectious as ever, despite even needing a feeding tube and catheter. He worked diligently with a therapist, hoping to regain some control of his left arm and leg, but it never happened.

"Life is actually very simple," he told Susan one day from his bed. "It's just difficult to remember that!"[4]

CROSSING OVER

Susan, two of their close friends, a few hospice nurses, and an Episcopal priest were the people who sat with him during his last days on Earth.

Doc's time was nearing. In the evening of that day, September 19, 2012, Kelsey and their three cats came into the room, almost simultaneously. Of the time, Susan wrote:

> When he made the transition, it was seamless. He was here and then he wasn't. He went from being with us, to being with God. It was heartbreaking to see those beautiful blue eyes closed, but his peacefulness filled the room. It was a quiet peace that settled upon our home and stayed there for many days. His Spirit left the body, but it was still in the house. I felt it as a very strong presence in the days after he died.[5]

Dr. David R. Hawkins was 85 years old. His body was washed and dressed in a traditional Korean burial garment that students from Dr. Moon's ashram in South Korea had made for him. Though generally this shroud would be white, for Doc, they had made a gold one in honor of his role as a great teacher. According to Dr. Hawkins's instruction, he was cremated three days after his death so that his body could adjust to the transition.

Though some of his ashes are interned at St. Andrew's, the local Episcopal church where Dr. Hawkins and Susan would attend services, the funeral took place at Trinity Episcopal Cathedral in Phoenix with 500 people in attendance, mostly students and other people who were touched by Doc's work. Traditional hymns were sung, and as part of the service, a bagpiper played "Taps" while a World War II veteran presented Susan with an American flag to honor his service in the navy.

"There is no such thing as actual death or dying," Doc wrote. "That is why we talked about letting go of the body and saying farewell to it because life goes to life; life never stops."[6]

AN ONGOING LEGACY

Though accolades never mattered to Dr. Hawkins, the many that he received during his lifetime share a picture of his journey. Dr. Hawkins received numerous recognitions for his scientific and humanitarian contributions, including: the Huxley Award for the "Inestimable Contribution to the Alleviation of Human Suffering"; Physician's Recognition Award by the American Medical Association; 50-Year Distinguished Life Fellow by the American Psychiatric Association; the Orthomolecular Medicine Hall of Fame; Who's Who in the World; and a nomination for the prestigious Templeton Prize, which honors progress in science and religion.

He qualified to become a member of Mensa in October of 1963. He was awarded an honorary doctor of divinity degree by the Church of Universal Brotherhood in 1969. In recognition of his contributions to humanity, he was knighted in 1996 by the Sovereign Order of the Hospitallers of St. John of Jerusalem by authority of the Priory of King Valdemar the Great. In 2000, he was bestowed the title "Tae Ryoung Sun Kak Tosa" (Teacher of Enlightenment).

Copies of *Letting Go: The Pathway of Surrender* arrived from the printer three weeks after Dr. Hawkins passed on—a reminder to Susan and all those left behind that it was okay to release their own emotional burdens about his passing. The work would continue on, offering truth and hope to students for years to come. Though his physical body passed on, his Spirit can be found in the books and recorded lectures he left behind.

Susan and the small team at Veritas Publishing and The Institute for Spiritual Research Inc. continue the stewardship of Dr. Hawkins's work. Their main goal is to preserve the words and messages so that when people encounter them, they have the full context of how Dr. Hawkins originally taught it. This is how the truth is passed on. And the truth that Doc wanted to share with the world was a message about love. Love is the path we must all travel. As Dr. Hawkins said in his very last lecture, "Lovingness is a way of being in the world, and that way, you light up the world."[7] Dr. David R. Hawkins certainly lit up the world for many people, and he will continue to do so for all who discover his work.

ACKNOWLEDGMENTS

Throughout the years, there have been many who have been a huge support to Dr. Hawkins's work. Without their assistance and love, many of the books, lectures, outside talks, research, and administrative duties would not have happened. Thank you all for your devotion, care, and help that you gave and continue to give to Dr. Hawkins and his work.

I am sure he is eternally grateful to be called (your) teacher of Enlightenment.

I would like to acknowledge:

- Wally and Kathy Arnold: for their long-standing friendship, encouragement, and assistance in so many ways.

- The Texas Study Group: who have helped to do extensive research for various book projects.

- Fran Grace: devoted student, editor, and writer for some of Dr. Hawkins's writings.

- Trailhead Video: from 2004 to 2012 video- and audiotaped Dr. Hawkins's live lectures for professional use.

- Gabe Valencia: dedicated friend and assistant to both David and me.

- Dr. Moon and the Korean Study Group: who often traveled out to Sedona with her students to attend the lectures, helped with live translating, and publishes Dr. Hawkins's books in Korean.

- Interlicense Inc.: who is our main contact responsible for the many contracts of foreign translations of Dr. Hawkins's books into many languages.

- Though we cannot name everyone individually: to the many staff members and volunteers of Veritas Publishing, who throughout the years worked tirelessly, lovingly, and efficiently to let people know about Dr. Hawkins through the Sedona lectures, outside travel talks, phone interviews, video and audio production, DVDs/CDs, photography, book publishing, shipping, stage security, and so much more.

- And to all the students and attendees throughout the world who have supported Veritas Publishing and The Institute for Spiritual Research Inc. through donations, purchases, study groups, and loving comments and letters, and continue to do so, I am deeply grateful to you all!

— **Susan Hawkins**
Gloria in Excelsis Deo!

THE MAP OF CONSCIOUSNESS®

God-view	Life-view	Level		Log	Emotion	Process
Self	Is	Enlightenment	⇧	700-1000	Ineffable	Pure Consciousness
All-Being	Perfect	Peace	⇧	600	Bliss	Illumination
One	Complete	Joy	⇧	540	Serenity	Transfiguration
Loving	Benign	Love	⇧	500	Reverence	Revelation
Wise	Meaningful	Reason	⇧	400	Understanding	Abstraction
Merciful	Harmonious	Acceptance	⇧	350	Forgiveness	Transcendence
Inspiring	Hopeful	Willingness	⇧	310	Optimism	Intention
Enabling	Satisfactory	Neutrality	⇧	250	Trust	Release
Permitting	Feasible	Courage	⇧⇩	200	Affirmation	Empowerment
Indifferent	Demanding	Pride	⇩	175	Scorn	Inflation
Vengeful	Antagonistic	Anger	⇩	150	Hate	Aggression
Denying	Disappointing	Desire	⇩	125	Craving	Enslavement
Punitive	Frightening	Fear	⇩	100	Anxiety	Withdrawal
Disdainful	Tragic	Grief	⇩	75	Regret	Despondency
Condemning	Hopeless	Apathy	⇩	50	Despair	Abdication
Vindictive	Evil	Guilt	⇩	30	Blame	Destruction
Despising	Miserable	Shame	⇩	20	Humiliation	Elimination

©The Institute for Spiritual Research, Inc. dba Veritas Publishing.
This chart cannot be reproduced.

ACCOMPLISHMENTS OF DR. DAVID R. HAWKINS

Education

- B.S., Marquette University, 1950
- M.D., Medical College of Wisconsin, 1953
- Internship, Columbia Hospital, 1953–1954
- New York School of Psychiatry, 1954–1957
- Psychoanalysis, 1956–1960

Private Interests

- Architecture
    - 16th-Century French: Researched, designed, and built 16th-century French country house and estate on north shore of Long Island, which attracted wide interest and acclaim for its design and execution.
    - Modern Energy-Free: Co-founded Space-Form Inc., which researched and designed underground dome housing for small communities—energy-free and ecologically balanced and so designed and placed on the land that the buildings are barely visible so

as to preserve the natural beauty of the land. Co-founded the Sedona Fellowship, which obtained 160 acres of remote property for the project.

- Spiritual Research
- Relief of Human Suffering
- Androgyny: On the Level of Consciousness

Memberships

- American Medical Association
- American Psychiatric Association
- New York State Medical Society
- Nassau County Medical Society
- Nassau Physicians' Guild
- Nassau Academy of Medicine
- New York Academy of Sciences
- American Association for the Advancement of Science
- New York State Psychiatric Association
- Qualified Psychiatrist, New York State Department of Mental Health
- Nassau Psychiatric Society
- New York State Clinical Directors Association
- American Association Psychiatric Administrators
- Academy of Orthomolecular Psychiatry (Founding President, Chairman of the Board)

Accomplishments of Dr. David R. Hawkins

- International Academy of Preventive Medicine
- American Holistic Health Association
- Huxley Institute for Biosocial Research (Board of Directors)
- Academy of Religion and Mental Health
- New York State Association of the Professions
- Academy of Psychosomatic Medicine
- Schizophrenia Foundation, New York State (Board of Directors, Medical Advisor)
- Schizophrenia Association of Long Island (Board of Directors, Medical Advisor)
- Attitudinal Healing Center of Long Island (Board of Directors, Medical Advisor)
- North Nassau Mental Health Center (Director Emeritus)
- Medical Society of the Brunswick Hospital (Director of Psychiatric Research)
- Attending Staff, Gracie Square Hospital
- Youth Consultation Services, Episcopal Diocese, Long Island (Psychiatric Consultant)
- Editorial Board, *Journal of Orthomolecular Psychiatry*
- Editorial Board, *Journal of Schizophrenia*
- Editorial Board (Alcoholism), *Journal of Psychotherapy*
- American Schizophrenia Association (Scientific Advisory Board)

- National Society for Autistic Children (Professional Advisory Board)
- Long Island Council on Alcoholism
- Federation of Mental Health Centers (Co-founder)
- American Medical Society on Alcoholism

Lectures, Courses, and Workshops on Consciousness, Spirituality, and Self-Healing Techniques

- Huxley Institute, Biltmore Hotel, Symposium (6/25/1973): Nutrient Therapy in Medicine
- State University at Farmingdale (5/4/1975): Mental Health in Action, Self-Help
- Queens College Health Fair (11/18/1975): Nutrition and Mental Health
- Queensborough Community Colleges (12/3/1975): Nutrition and Mental Health
- North Nassau Mental Health Center (5/2/1976): Biochemistry of Mental Illness
- Schizophrenia Foundation of San Francisco, Sacramento, Oakland, St. Louis, and Cambridge by Mr. Shriftman and Video (3/1976)
- Canadian Schizophrenia Association's Fifth Annual Conference, Winnipeg (5/5/1976): Diagnosis of Schizophrenia
- Youth Consultation Services of Long Island (5/15/1976): Nutrition and Mental Health

Accomplishments of Dr. David R. Hawkins

- Special Days in May (5/16/1976): Fundraising Address for Mental Health
- New York Holistic Health Center Association (1976): Ortho Concepts
- University of Connecticut, Hartford
- Connecticut Mutual Life Insurance Company
- Academy of Orthomolecular Psychiatry (7/9/1976): Politics of Nutrition and Mental Health
- Long Island Schizophrenia Association (10/22/1976): Nutrition and Mental Illness
- Academy of Orthomolecular Psychiatry (8/24/1977): Phoenix
- New York Association of Holistic Health Centers (5/1978)
- United States Senate Hearings on Nutrition (McGovern's Committee Special Hearings) Washington, D.C. (5/12/1978)
- Center for the Healing Arts, New York (6/28/1978): Biochemistry and the Treatment of Mental Illness
- Attitudinal Healing Center of Long Island (1979–1983): Seminars for Group Facilitators
- Miracles Study Groups, Long Island, New York, Arizona, California, and other states (1979–1983): Lectures on Scientific Demonstration by Kinesiology of the Clinical Proof of the Power of *A Course in Miracles*

- Workshops in New York and Arizona (1979–1983): Rebirthing Techniques
- Institute for Applied Spiritual Studies (1979–1984): Numerous lectures and small group workshops on meditation and consciousness techniques to increase spiritual growth and awareness
- Unity Church, Sedona, Arizona (12/1979): *A Course in Miracles*
- Institute for Applied Spiritual Studies, Sedona, Arizona (1980–1982): Releasing Workshops
- Unity Church, Sedona, Arizona (1980–1982): Conducted classes on *A Course in Miracles* and Metaphysics
- Sedona School, Sedona, Arizona (1980–1982): Weekly classes on *A Course in Miracles*
- Sedona Church of Light (1980–1981): Weekly classes on *A Course in Miracles*
- Unity Church, Sedona, Arizona (1/15/1980): Sermon: The Power of Forgiveness in Self-Healing
- Academy of Orthomolecular Psychiatry (5/5/1980): A Preventive Measure for Tardive Dyskinesia
- Spiritual Awareness and Consciousness Techniques in Self-Healing Workshops in Puerto Vallarta, Mexico (1981–1984): Quarterly, small groups
- Scottsdale Hilton (2/23/1981): Stress Reduction

Accomplishments of Dr. David R. Hawkins

- Pointe Resort, Scottsdale (2/24/1981): Self-Healing by Use of the Releasing Method
- Metro Center, Phoenix (2/25/1981): Stress Reduction by the Sedona Releasing Method
- Radisson Racquet Club (2/26/81): The Sedona Releasing Method and Self-Healing
- Northeastern Regional Conference, *A Course in Miracles*, Barbizon-Plaza Hotel, New York (5/2/1981): Forgiveness and Self-Healing
- Arizona State AA Roundup, Sedona, Arizona (6/6/1981): Recovery from Alcoholism
- Phoenix Ad Club (6/22/1981): Stress Reduction and Self-Healing by Use of the Releasing Consciousness Techniques
- King's Ransom Inn, Sedona, Arizona (6/27/1981): The Sedona Releasing Method and Self-Healing
- Institute for Applied Spiritual Studies (10/1981): Personal Transformational Counselor Seminars
- Cairo, Egypt, (11/1981): Lecture Series on *A Course in Miracles*
- Academy of Orthomolecular Psychiatry (5/5/1984): The Prevention of Tardive Dyskinesia—A Survey of 50,000 Patients Treated by Orthomolecular Psychiatry
- Northeastern Regional Conference, *A Course in Miracles*, Barbizon-Plaza Hotel, New York (5/22–23/1982): Scientific Proof of the Effect of *A Course in Miracles*

- Sedona Flicker Shack (3/21/1982): Attitudinal Healing with Jerry Jampolsky, M.D.
- Western Regional Conference, *A Course in Miracles*, San Francisco (3/5–6/1983): Reshaping Our World
- Bridgebuilders, Detroit (6/10/1983): Self-Healing
- Michigan State University (6/11/1983): Spiritual Awareness and Self-Healing Workshops
- Western Regional Conference, *A Course in Miracles*, Los Angeles (3/31/1984): Spiritual Awareness and Self-Healing

TV and Radio Appearances

- WHLI—New York, NY (9/4/1963): Recovery from Mental Illness
- WLIR—New York, NY (11/1963): Alcoholism, Drug Addiction
- WOR—New York, NY, *Barry Farber Show* (1967): Multiple appearances
- IEVB—New York, NY, *Lee Steiner Show* (1968): Multiple appearances
- Carleton Fredericks (1968–1972): Multiple appearances
- WNEW—New York, NY, Channel 5 (1969): Nutrition and Mental Health

Accomplishments of Dr. David R. Hawkins

- KCOP—Los Angeles, CA, Channel 13, Labor Report (6/13/1970): Orthomolecular Psychiatry
- PBS—New York, NY, channel 13 (6/22–23/1970): Mental Health
- NBC—New York, NY, *Not For Women Only*, Barbara Walters (1/11–15/1971): Mental Health
- CBS—New York, NY, Channel 2, Walter Cronkite (2/11/1971): Orthomolecular Psychiatry
- ABC—A.M. New York, NY, Channel 7, *John Bartholomew Tucker Show* (2/16/1971): Mental Disorders
- WMCA—New York, NY, *Fred Gale Show* (3/24/1971)
- National Education TV Film: Schizophrenia
- WNBC (1/16/1972): Schizophrenia
- WNBC (7/22/1972): Service Report with Frank Fields
- TV Network for Continuing Medical Education: Psychiatry '73
- WEEI—Boston, MA (3/27/1973): Orthomolecular Psychiatry
- CBS—Boston, MA, Channel 4 (6/15/1973): Nutrition and Mental Health
- CBS—Boston, MA, Channel 4 (6/22/1973): Schizophrenia

- WTFM—New York, NY (12/1973–1/1974): 11 programs on multiple subjects of mental health
- WOR—New York, NY (2/26/1974): Mental Health
- WOR—New York, NY, *Pat McCann Show* (2/26, 3/19/1974): Nutrition and Mental Health
- NBC—New York, NY, *Not For Women Only*, Barbara Walters (4/20, 4/29, 5/1/1974): Orthomolecular Psychiatry
- *The Mid-Day Show*, Gwen Verdon (5/2/1974): New Approaches to Mental Health
- WHPC-FM—New York, NY (5/20/74): Nutrition and Mental Health
- WRVR-FM—New York, NY, *Metroscope*: Hypoglycemia
- CBS—Roanoke, VA (5/23/1974): Orthomolecular Psychiatry
- NBC—New York, NY, *Not For Women Only*, Barbara Walters (8/26, 8/27, 8/30/1974): Nutrition and Mental Health
- NBC—New York, NY, *Not For Women Only* Barbara Walters (6/22/1976)
- WOR—New York, NY, *Pat McCann Show* (3/8/1977): Hypoglycemia
- *MacNeil/Lehrer Report* (6/22/1977): Orthomolecular Psychiatry
- New York, NY, Channel 2, *Straight Talk* (8/1977): Mental Illness

- Phoenix, AZ, Phoenix TV (1981): Stress Reduction
- Flagstaff, AZ, Channel 2 (1981): Stress Reduction
- San Francisco, CA, New Dimensions Radio FM, Mike Thon (1981): The Sedona Releasing Method
- WGBB—New York, NY, *Ray Heatherton Show* (1982–1983): Multiple appearances on Consciousness Techniques to Improve Health and Reduce Stress
- WKTN—Pittsburgh, PA (1982–1983): Multiple appearances on Consciousness and Spiritual Techniques to Improve Health and Reduce Stress
- Plus many others across the United States and Canada

Awards, Recognitions, and Life Events

- Honor Camper of the Year Award (1941)
- Alpha Omega Alpha—National Medical Scholastic Honor Society (1952)
- Mosby Book Award for Scholastic Excellence (1953)
- Intern of the Year (1954)
- Awarded Fellowship at Mount Sinai Hospital in Psychiatry (1956)
- Supervising Psychiatrist by competitive statewide exam (1957)

- Director, Mental Health Clinic (1958)
- Accepted for four-year psychoanalysis training at Columbia University Psychoanalytic Clinic
- North Nassau Mental Health Center Award for Alleviation of Human Suffering (1978)
- Huxley Award for Inestimable Contribution to the Alleviation of Human Suffering (1979)
- Citation from Medical College of Wisconsin for Contributions to Medicine
- Invited to become Commissioner of Mental Health, State of New York (1983)
- Discovered the preventive cure for tardive dyskinesia, an irreversible, crippling neurological disease for which there has been no cure or prevention. According to a CBS documentary on the subject, it is predicted that it will afflict one million Americans within a few years. The discovery that it is almost 100 percent preventable was the result of a study Dr. Hawkins completed on 58,000 patients. This is a major discovery, as tardive dyskinesia is the most difficult enigma facing psychiatry today.

Founded

- North Nassau Psychiatric Center (1958)
- Mental Health Center, Inc.
- Federation of Mental Health Centers (1963)
- North Nassau Clinical Laboratories (1970)

Accomplishments of Dr. David R. Hawkins

- North Nassau Research Division and Laboratories (1971)
- An Integrated System for the Care of Schizophrenics (1971)
- The Academy of Orthomolecular Psychiatry (1971)
- Institute for Applied Spiritual Studies (1980)
- Sedona Fellowship (1981)
- Institute for Applied Spiritual Studies, Inc. (1983)

Co-founded

- Schizophrenics Anonymous (Medical Advisor & Board of Directors)
- Schizophrenia Foundation of New York State (Incorporator and Director)
- Schizophrenia Foundation of Long Island (Medical Advisor and Board of Directors)
- The Institute for Scientific Communications (Incorporator and Board of Directors)
- *Journal of Orthomolecular Psychiatry* (Editorial Board)
- *Journal of Schizophrenia* (Editorial Board)
- St. George's Day Activities Center (Medical Advisor)
- Attitudinal Healing Center of Long Island (Medical Advisor and Board of Directors)

- Christ Church Day Activities Center (Medical Advisor)
- The Masters Gallery of Fine Arts (Co-director)
- Mental Health Fairs
- Gateposts (Halfway House) (Medical Advisor)
- Garfield House (Halfway House)
- Day Activities Center of Port Washington (Medical Advisor)
- Brunswick House (Alcoholism) (Psychiatric Consultant)
- New York Association of Holistic Health Centers
- Life Support Systems, Inc. (Incorporator and Board of Directors)

Recognized in

- *Who's Who in the East*
- *Biographical Directory of American Psychological Association*
- *Dictionary of International Biography,* Vol. 4
- *American Men of Medicine*
- *Distinguished Americans*
- *National Social Directory*
- *The Blue Book*
- *Directory of English and American Writers*

Memberships

- Brunswick House (Director of Research, Alcoholism)

Accomplishments of Dr. David R. Hawkins

- National Acupuncture Research Society
- American Geriatric Society
- International Council of Applied Nutrition
- Academy of Preventive Medicine
- Canadian Psychiatric Association
- American Society for Psychological Research
- Monroe Institute for Applied Science
- International Kirlian Research Association
- National Council on Alcoholism
- The Association for the Advancement of Psychotherapy
- Society for the Study of Addictions
- American Institute for Scientific Communications (Co-founder)
- International Society for General Semantics
- Consultant on Alcoholism, U.S. Department of Health, Education, and Welfare
- American Orthoanalytic Association
- Consultant, New York Foundling Hospital
- New York Paleontological Society
- International Platform Association
- Consultant, CSD Rescue Service
- Consultant, Operation Hotline
- Non-Medical
  - Institute for Applied Spiritual Studies (Founder and Chairman)
  - Sedona Fellowship (President and Co-founder)

- Sedona Institute (Medical Consultant)
- Rogers Williams Society (Descendant)
- Mensa
- Association for Research and Enlightenment
- First Zen Institute of America (Member since 1960)
- Sedona Self-Realization Groups

Publications

- "The Incidence & Clinical Significance of Hemoptysis," *Marquette Medical Review* (1952)
- "Cancer of the Lower Colon," *Marquette Medical Review* (1953)
- "Electro-Shock Technique," *American Journal of Psychiatry* (May 1958)
- "Advantages to the Psychiatric Clinic of the HOD Test," *Schizophrenia* (1967)
- "Practical Application of the Results of Biochemical Research in Every Day Clinical Practices," Proceedings, Scientific Advisory Committee, American Schizophrenia Foundation (January 1967)
- "Treatment of Schizophrenia Based on the Medical Model," *Journal of Schizophrenia* (1968)
- "Treatment of Out-Patient Schizophrenics & Schizophrenic-Alcoholics Based on the Medical Model," *The Vitamin B-3 Therapy: A Second Communication to A.A.'s Physicians*, edited by Bill Wilson (February 1968)

- "Further Observations on the Biochemical Treatment of Schizophrenia and Its Relationship to the Field of Orthomolecular Psychiatry," Schizophrenia Foundation, New York (May 1968)
- "The B3 Therapy," edited by Bill Wilson (1969)
- "Schizophrenia: Response to Intensive Hospital Treatment as Monitored by the HOD and OIT Test," *Schizophrenia* (1969)
- "Psychotherapy vs. Chemotherapy," in *The Treatment of Schizophrenia*, American Schizophrenia Foundation (January 1969)
- "The Use of the HOD Test in a Busy Out-Patient Clinic," in *The HOD Test in Medical Practice*, edited by H. Keim (1970)
- "Orthomolecular Psychiatry," *Psychosomatics* (1970)
- "An Integrated Community System for the Effective Treatment of Schizophrenia," *Schizophrenia* (1971)
- "Orthomolecular Psychiatry: Treatment, Alcoholism," supplement to *The Vitamin B-3 Therapy: A Third Communication to A.A.'s Physicians*, edited by Bill Wilson (1971)
- Schizophrenia, Research Project, NBC Science Public Affairs (1972)
- Preface to *Megavitamin Therapy* (1973)
- *Orthomolecular Psychiatry*, co-edited by L. Pauling (1973)

- "Orthomolecular Psychiatry," Executive Health (October 1975)
- "Community Involvement in Orthomolecular Psychiatry," *Journal of Orthomolecular Psychiatry* (1976)
- "Attitudes on Approaches to the Difficult Patient," Proceedings, Long Island Schizophrenia Foundation (May 1976)
- "Ortomolekylar Psykiatri" *Observanda Medica* (in Swedish) (June 1976)
- "Schizophrenics Anonymous," World Medical News, Diagnosing the Schizophrenias, *Journal of Orthomolecular Psychiatry* (1977)
- Forword to *The Food/Depression Connection*, June Roth (1978)
- "Some Thoughts on Balancing Body Chemistry," *Release* (December 1981)
- "A Preventive Measure for Tardive Dyskinesia" with C. Tkacz, *Journal of Orthomolecular Psychiatry* (1982)
- "The Potential Value of Specifics in the Nutritional Treatment of Schizophrenia" with C. Tkacz, Academy of Orthomolecular Psychiatry (May 1982)
- "Orthomolecular Psychiatry," in *International Encyclopedia of Psychiatry, Psychoanalysis and Psychology*

- "Prevention of Tardive Dyskinesia by High Dose Vitamins," Academy of Orthomolecular Psychiatry, (May 1984)
- Introduction to *Diet Away Your Stress, Tension, and Anxiety: The Fructose Diet*, J. Daniel Palm (1976)
- Abstracts on Alcoholism, *American Journal of Psychotherapy* (1968–1973)
  - "Psychoanalytic Views on Alcoholism"
  - "Growth of A.A. in a Southeastern City"
  - "The Fate of Untreated Alcoholics"
  - "A Multi-Disciplinary Approach to Alcoholism"
  - "Hypnotic Treatment of Various Forms of Addiction"
  - "Alcoholic Values in A.A."
  - "Alcoholism Prevention and Reality"
  - "The Concept of Motivation in the Treatment of Alcoholics"
  - "Management of the Alcoholic in an Acute Treatment Facility"
  - "Evaluation of Treatments for Alcohol Withdrawal Syndrome"
  - "The Effect of Attitudes in the Therapy of the Alcoholic"
  - "Experimental Analysis of Alcoholic Drinking Patterns"
  - "Management of Acute Alcohol Withdrawal States"
- Book Reviews, *American Journal of Psychotherapy*
  - *How to Live with an Alcoholic*

- *Alcoholism*
- *The Drinker's Addiction*

Publications on Non-Medical Topics: Spirituality

- "On Love" (multiple issue series), *Miracle News* (1981–1983)
- "The Doctor: On Love," *Miracle Digest* (1983)
- "Love," *Call of the Canyon* (1982)
- "Peace," *Call of the Canyon* (1982)
- "Gratitude," *Call of the Canyon* (1982)
- "Expanding Love," *Call of the Canyon* (2/1982)
- "Dr. Love," *Call of the Canyon* (6/1982)
- "Beauty," *Call of the Canyon* (1983)
- "Silence," *Call of the Canyon* (1983)
- "Joy," *Call of the Canyon* (1983)
- "Metamorphosis," four issues, *Call of the Canyon* (1984)
- "The Sedona Method" (two-hour cassette tape #1573 from New Dimensions Radio)
- "Self-Healing" (four-hour cassette workshop, available from Coleman Graphics)
- "Operational Synopsis of *A Course in Miracles*," Western Conference, Los Angeles (3/31/1984)

Accomplishments of Dr. David R. Hawkins

Lectures

- North Nassau Mental Health Center (1958–1981): Over 100 lectures on all aspects of mental illness
- Federation of Mental Health Centers (1960–1963): Presidential addresses
- Schizophrenics Anonymous of New York (9/26/1962) with Dr. Ruth Fox and Bill Wilson
- E. I. DuPont de Nemours and Company (4/2/1963): "New Concepts in Mental Health: Alcoholism"
- Louisiana State University (5/27/1963): "New Treatments in Mental Illness"
- Brunswick Hospital (1967–1979): Multiple lectures on all aspects of mental illness, lecture series on Research in Psychiatry
- Brunswick Hospital, Scientific Advisory Board of the American Schizophrenia Foundation (1/21–22/1967)
- The Institute for Scientific Communications (4/15/1967): Presidential address
- Trinity Church, New York, NY (9/26/1967): "The Founding of Schizophrenics Anonymous"
- University of Michigan, Ann Arbor (10/23/1967): "New Treatments for Mental Illness"
- Al-Anon meetings, multiple throughout the United States (1968–1979): "Recovery from Alcoholism"

- Fordham University (1/13/1968): "Schizophrenic's Response to Intensive Treatment"
- Hotel Americana, New York, NY (4/22/1968): American Schizophrenia Association
- Fordham University (4/22/1968): "Biologic Factors and Schizophrenia"
- Schizophrenia Foundation of Connecticut (4/22/1968): "Schizophrenia, Diagnosis and Newer Treatments"
- Guest House, Detroit, MI (9/1968), with Bill Wilson, founder of AA: "Hypoglycemia, Metavitamins and Alcoholism"
- Family Counseling and Youth Services, Episcopal Diocese of Long Island (1969–1979): Multiple lectures on all aspects of mental health
- Schizophrenics Anonymous of Connecticut (6/15/1969)
- Syosset Hospital (10/13/1968): "Megavitamins and Hypoglycemia"
- Schizophrenia Foundation of Greater Washington (3/27/1969): "Treatment of Schizophrenia"
- Great Neck Synagogue (10/14/1969): "Mental Health"
- Long Island Jewish Hospital (10/16/1969): "Treatment of the Difficult Patient"
- Schizophrenia Foundation of New York (10/21/1969): "Treatment of Schizophrenia"

Accomplishments of Dr. David R. Hawkins

- New York Medical College Hospitals (1/31/1969): "Biologic Treatment of Schizophrenia"
- Alcoholics Anonymous, World Headquarters, New York City, Board of Directors (4/1969): "Nutritional Concepts in the Treatment of Alcoholism"
- Kings County Hospital (4/10/1969): "Biological Treatment in Psychiatry"
- E. I. DuPont de Nemours and Company (4/11/1969): "New Concepts in Mental Health: Alcoholism"
- Armstrong Cork Company (9/9/1969): "Nutrition and Mental Health"
- City of New York General Psychiatric Clinic (5/2/1969): "New Concepts in Psychiatric Treatment"
- Queens County Mental Health Clinic (6/13/1969): "New Concepts"
- Schizophrenia Foundation of Washington (10/19/1969): "Treatment of Schizophrenics and Alcoholism in a Mental Health Center"
- Nassau Academy of Medicine (11/3/1969): "Biochemical Aspects of Schizophrenia"
- Schizophrenia Association of Long Island (12/16/1969): "The Hippie Scene, Psychiatric Drugs and Schizophrenia"

- Long Island Council on Alcoholism: "Hypoglycemia and Megavitamins in the Treatment of Alcoholism"
- Kingman Hall, New York: "Soft Drug Addiction"
- Recovery, Inc., 10th Avenue, New York: "The Clinical Value of the Recovery Self-Help Groups"
- Operation Hotline, New York: "Drug Crisis"
- LSD Reserve Service, New York: "Drug Crisis"
- Huxley Institute, Annual Conference on Biological Aspects of Psychiatry (1970)
- Schizophrenia Foundations of Alameda County, San Francisco, Iowa, North Carolina, Virginia, Maine, Seattle, New Jersey, Baltimore, Winnipeg, Calgary, and others (1970–1974)
- Webber Pharmaceuticals, Toronto, Board of Directors Meetings (1970–1974): "New Advances in Nutrition"
- The Academy of Psychosomatic Medicine (1/12/1970): "Orthomolecular Psychiatry"
- Sociedad Argentina de Medicina Psicosomática (1/15/1970): "Orthomolecular Psychiatry"
- National Society for Autistic Children (3/19/1970): "Orthomolecular Psychiatry"
- Episcopal Charities Appeal of Long Island (4/28/1970)

- Salisbury Club, Long Island, New York (4/28/1970): "Hopeful New Approaches"
- Schizophrenia Foundation of New York (5/21/1970): "Recent Development in the Treatment of Schizophrenia"
- Community Church, New York (5/21/1970): "Mental Health"
- Cancer Research Hospital, Boston (5/27/1970): "Schizophrenia Foundations"
- Harvard University, Fund Aud., Schiz. Association of Mass. (5/27/1970): "An Alternate Approach to the Treatment of Schizophrenia"
- Retail Clerks Union, AFL-CIO, Los Angeles Hilton (6/13/1970): "Orthomolecular Psychiatry"
- Christ Church, Long Island, New York (7/7/1970): "Emergency Drug Crises"
- Festival of Life, Long Island, New York (8/25/1970): "Drug Crisis"
- Stanford University, California (9/1970): "Department of Orthomolecular Medicine and Megavitamins"
- Waterbury Hospital, Connecticut (9/29/1970): "New Treatment Concepts"
- Eisenhower Park, Youth Conference (10/29/1970): "Drug Problems"
- Schizophrenia Association of Long Island (10/29/1970, 12/15/1970): "Approaches to

Schizophrenia That Offer Hope to Patients and Their Families"
- Miami Heart Institute (11/15/1970): "Biochemical Aspects of Alcoholism"
- Town of Hampstead (11/16/1970): "Community Drug Problems"
- Nassau Hospital, New York (11/17/1970): "Hypoglycemia and Psychiatry"
- Nassau Hospital (12/15/1970): "Treatment of Schizophrenia"
- Nassau Hospital (2/9/1971): "The Uncooperative Patient"
- University of Alabama (3/8/1972): "Orthomolecular Psychiatry"
- American Schizophrenia Association, Harvard Club, New York (4/2/1971): "An Integrated Community System for the Treatment of Schizophrenia"
- Meadowbrook Hospital, Long Island, New York (4/14/1971): "Orthomolecular Psychiatry"
- Board of Trustees of Alcoholics Anonymous (4/24/1971): "Research"
- Joint Meeting of the Schizophrenia Associations of Great Britain, Canada, and the United States, London (9/28/1971)
- Founding Meeting, Academy of Orthomolecular Psychiatry, Dean's Yard, Westminster Abbey (9/29/1971): Presidential address

Accomplishments of Dr. David R. Hawkins

- State University of New York, Post College (10/10/1971): "Self Help Groups, People in Action"
- Bangor Counseling Center, Maine (12/3/1971): "Orthomolecular Psychiatry"
- Pine Tree Schizophrenia Association (12/3/1971): "Treatment of Schizophrenia"
- Academy of Orthomolecular Psychiatry, Dallas (4/28/1972): Presidential address
- State University of New York (5/7/1972): "Mental Health in Action: Self-Help Groups"
- City University of New York (10/22/1972): "Mental Health in Action, Self-Help Groups"
- North Nassau Mental Health Center (12/17/1972): "Advanced Techniques in Diagnosis and Treatment"
- Queensborough Community College (3/28/1973): "Hypoglycemia, Alcoholism, Drug Addiction"
- Christ Church, Manhasset, New York (4/18/1973): "Mental Health Clinics"
- Huxley Institute for Biosocial Research, Biltmore Hotel, New York (4/20/1973): "Biological Aspects of Mental Illness"
- Academy of Orthomolecular Psychiatry, Detroit (5/3/1973): Presidential address
- Third Annual Conference, Canadian Schizophrenic Association, Vancouver, B.C. (6/1973): "Orthomolecular Psychiatry"

- State University of New York (6/5/1973): "Alcoholism"
- Hunter College, CUNY (10/15/1973): "Orthomolecular Psychiatry"
- C. W. Post College, Graduate School (11/7/1973): "Nutrition and Human Behavior"
- Schizophrenia Foundation of St. Louis (12/1973): "New Treatments for Schizophrenia"
- Nassau County Medical Center (12/9/1973): "Nutrition and Human Behavior"
- Brunswick Hospital Annual Medical Conference (6/15/1974): "Alcoholism and Cross Addiction"
- Hofstra College (4/23/1974): "Treatment of Violent Behavior"
- Brunswick Hospital (6/6/1974): "Psychiatry"
- International Academy of Metabiology (6/15/1974): "Cerebral Allergy"
- Long Island Schizophrenia Association, Fifth Annual Symposium (10/23/1974): "Research"
- New York Institute of Technology, Health Fair

SUMMARY OF BOOKS BY DR. DAVID R. HAWKINS

Orthomolecular Psychiatry: Treatment of Schizophrenia (co-editor, 1973)

A pioneering work that challenges conventional psychiatric approaches to schizophrenia, the book introduces the concept of orthomolecular medicine, proposing that mental disorders, particularly schizophrenia, can be effectively treated by optimizing the biochemical environment of the body through the use of natural substances. The authors advocate for the administration of therapeutic doses of vitamins, particularly vitamin B3 (niacin), as a fundamental component of treatment. They argue that deficiencies in certain nutrients contribute to the manifestation and exacerbation of mental illnesses, and correcting these imbalances can lead to significant improvements in symptoms and overall well-being.

The book delves into case studies and clinical experiences, presenting evidence to support the effectiveness of orthomolecular approaches in treating schizophrenia. The authors detail the biochemical rationale behind their recommendations, emphasizing the role of nutrition in mental health. The authors also discuss the potential benefits of other nutrients, such as vitamin C and essential fatty acids, in complementing the treatment of schizophrenia. While controversial at the time, *Orthomolecular Psychiatry* has had a lasting impact, influencing subsequent research and contributing to the ongoing dialogue about the role of nutrition in mental health and the holistic treatment of psychiatric disorders.

Despite the initial skepticism from the mainstream medical community, the book has inspired further exploration of nutritional interventions in mental health and has paved the way for the integration of orthomolecular approaches into holistic psychiatric care. The enduring relevance of *Orthomolecular Psychiatry* lies in its challenge to the traditional biomedical model and its advocacy for a more comprehensive understanding of mental health that incorporates nutritional and biochemical considerations.

Power vs. Force: The Hidden Determinants of Human Behavior (1994)

Power vs. Force is a groundbreaking exploration of the intricacies of human consciousness and its profound impact on our lives. At the heart of this transformative work is the introduction of the Map of Consciousness®, a comprehensive scale that categorizes emotions, thoughts, and states of being according to their energetic frequencies. Hawkins assigns numerical values to various levels of consciousness, ranging from the lowest, characterized by shame and guilt, to the highest, symbolized by pure enlightenment.

The key premise of the book revolves around the stark difference between power and force. Hawkins argues that genuine power, emanating from higher states of consciousness, such as love, integrity, and wisdom, holds an intrinsic and enduring influence. In contrast, force, which relies on manipulation, coercion, and aggression, is fleeting and ultimately ineffective. The book challenges readers to reevaluate their understanding of power, urging them to move beyond the limitations of ego-driven forces and tap into the transformative potential of higher consciousness.

Hawkins seamlessly blends scientific inquiry with spiritual insights, offering a unique synthesis that appeals to a broad audience. By emphasizing the significance of cultivating elevated states of awareness, the book becomes a road map for personal growth, encouraging readers to transcend their self-imposed limitations and unlock the inherent power within. *Power vs. Force* has left an indelible mark on the fields of spirituality and self-help, providing a profound and practical guide for individuals seeking positive transformation and a deeper understanding of the interplay between consciousness and the human experience.

The Eye of the I: From Which Nothing Is Hidden (2001)

Building upon the foundation laid in his first book, Dr. Hawkins delves deeper into the nature of consciousness, enlightenment, and the transformative journey toward self-realization. The title metaphorically refers to an elevated state of awareness, often associated with the "I" or the true self, from which nothing remains hidden, and all aspects of existence are illuminated.

The book introduces the concept of calibrated levels of consciousness, expanding on the Map of Consciousness® presented in *Power vs. Force*. Hawkins elucidates the characteristics of various levels, from shame and guilt to unconditional love and enlightenment. He discusses the challenges and revelations experienced at each stage, providing insights into the human condition and the potential for spiritual evolution.

Hawkins incorporates personal anecdotes, philosophical reflections, and spiritual teachings to guide readers on a contemplative journey. The book encourages individuals to embrace a path of higher consciousness, shedding the limitations of the ego, and realizing the interconnectedness of all life. *The Eye of the I* serves as a profound and introspective guide, inviting readers to explore the depths of their own consciousness and discover the unifying thread that connects every aspect of the human experience.

I: Reality and Subjectivity (2003)

The third book in the unofficial trilogy of masterworks, *I* is the culmination of a comprehensive exploration of consciousness and the nature of reality. Hawkins delves deeper into metaphysical and philosophical concepts. The book delves into the interplay between reality and subjectivity, inviting readers to contemplate the nature of perception, the self, and the ultimate reality.

One of the central themes of the book is the exploration of the levels of consciousness, expanding on the Scale of Consciousness introduced in earlier works. Hawkins provides a nuanced understanding of the calibrated levels, discussing the characteristics and implications of each stage on the spiritual journey. The book emphasizes the transformative power of higher states of consciousness, advocating for the dissolution of the ego and the recognition of one's true nature.

Hawkins blends spiritual teachings, scientific insights, and personal reflections to offer a multidimensional perspective on reality and subjectivity. The book serves as a guide for individuals seeking a deeper understanding of their own consciousness and its relationship to the broader universe.

I: Reality and Subjectivity continues Hawkins's exploration of the human experience, providing a road map for those on a quest for self-realization and a more profound connection with the infinite and eternal aspects of reality.

Truth vs. Falsehood: How to Tell the Difference (2005)

Building upon the muscle testing introduced in *Power vs. Force*, Hawkins expands on applied kinesiology, which he employs as a tool to discern truth from falsehood. The book explores the calibrated levels of consciousness, presenting a Scale of Truth that ranges from falsehood to the highest levels of spiritual truth.

Hawkins examines various aspects of life, from emotions and relationships to historical events and religious doctrines, assigning calibrated values to each based on their truthfulness. He contends that higher levels of consciousness are associated with truth and integrity, while lower levels are linked to falsehood and deception. The book also delves into the impact of truth on individual and collective well-being, emphasizing the transformative power of aligning with higher states of consciousness.

Throughout the book, Hawkins weaves together spiritual insights, scientific principles, and practical applications of the muscle testing technique. *Truth vs. Falsehood* serves as a guide for readers seeking to navigate the complexities of life, make informed decisions, and cultivate a deeper understanding of the universal truths that underpin existence. The book invites individuals to explore the relationship between consciousness and truth, offering valuable insights into the nature of reality and the pursuit of higher awareness.

Transcending the Levels of Consciousness: The Stairway to Enlightenment (2006)

Utilizing the Map of Consciousness®, Dr. Hawkins provides a detailed road map for individuals seeking higher states of awareness. The book delves into the calibrated levels of consciousness, each representing a unique stage on the path to enlightenment, from the lower levels characterized by shame and guilt to the highest levels associated with unconditional love and enlightenment.

Hawkins explores the dynamics of spiritual growth, shedding light on the challenges and opportunities at each stage of the journey. He emphasizes the transformative power of love, forgiveness, and surrender in elevating consciousness. The concept of kinesiology and muscle testing is incorporated as a practical tool for individuals to discern their own levels of consciousness and make choices that align with their spiritual goals.

Throughout the book, Hawkins blends spiritual teachings, psychological insights, and practical guidance to provide a comprehensive understanding of the stairway to enlightenment. *Transcending the Levels of Consciousness* serves as an inspiring and instructive resource for those seeking a deeper connection with their true selves and the universal consciousness. It encourages readers to transcend the limitations of the ego, embrace higher states of awareness, and embark on a transformative journey toward spiritual enlightenment.

Discovery of the Presence of God: Devotional Nonduality (2006)

Moving in a different direction from his previous works, within this book is a profound exploration of spirituality, blending the principles of devotional practices with the concept of nonduality. The book invites readers into a deep contemplation of the divine presence and the intimate connection between the individual and the universal consciousness. Drawing on his extensive background in psychiatry and spiritual teachings, Hawkins provides insights into the nature of God, love, and the transformative power of devotional practices.

At the heart of the book is the exploration of the concept of devotional nonduality, emphasizing the merger of individual consciousness with the divine through love, surrender, and devotion. Hawkins discusses various devotional practices and their potential to elevate one's level of consciousness. The book encourages readers to go beyond intellectual understanding and embrace a heart-centered approach to spirituality.

Discovery of the Presence of God serves as both a guide and an inspiration for individuals on the spiritual path. Through personal anecdotes, teachings, and practical advice, Hawkins navigates the reader through the terrain of devotion, leading to the profound discovery of the omnipresent and transcendent nature of God. The book offers a unique perspective on the interplay between devotional practices and the realization of nondual awareness, fostering a deeper understanding of the divine presence in every aspect of life.

Reality, Spirituality, and Modern Man (2008)

Offering an expansive exploration of spiritual principles and their application in the context of contemporary life, the focus of this work is the evolution of the human spirit. The book delves into the challenges faced by modern individuals in navigating the complexities of the material world while seeking higher states of consciousness.

Using muscle testing as a practical tool for discerning truth and calibrating levels of consciousness, he emphasizes the transformative power of spiritual practices, including prayer, meditation, and surrender, in elevating individual consciousness. The book also addresses the impact of societal influences, cultural conditioning, and the media on the collective consciousness of modern humanity.

Throughout the book, Hawkins weaves together scientific insights, spiritual teachings, and practical guidance. He explores the role of intention, integrity, and love in the process of spiritual awakening. *Reality, Spirituality, and Modern Man* serves as a guide for individuals seeking to integrate spiritual principles into their daily lives and navigate the challenges of the modern world with a heightened awareness of the spiritual dimension. The book offers a holistic perspective on reality and spirituality, bridging the gap between ancient wisdom and contemporary understanding.

Healing and Recovery (2009)

This book was the result of a group of lectures given by the author at the request of the original publisher of *A Course in Miracles*, along with members of several self-help groups, including Alcoholics Anonymous, ACIM, Attitudinal Healing Centers, other recovery groups, and a number of clinicians.

Our society lives with constant stress, anxiety, fear, pain, suffering, depression, and worry. Alcoholism, drug addiction, obesity, sexual problems, and cancer are constantly in the news. Mankind in general has had very little information about how to address life's challenges without resorting to drugs, surgery, or counseling. Hawkins unpacks why the body may not respond to traditional medical approaches.

Specific instructions and guidelines are provided that can result in complete healing from any disease. The importance of including spiritual practices in one's healing and recovery program is explained, along with how easy it is to incorporate them in the process.

Healing and Recovery provides clinically proven self-healing methods that will enable you to take charge of your health and live a happy, healthy, and fulfilling life.

Letting Go: The Pathway of Surrender (2012)

A profound exploration of the transformative journey toward emotional and spiritual freedom. Dr. Hawkins introduces the concept of surrender as a potent tool for releasing deeply rooted emotions, attachments, and conditioned responses that can hinder personal growth. The book emphasizes that embracing surrender is not a sign of weakness but a courageous and empowering choice that opens the door to higher states of consciousness.

Central to the book is the idea that emotions are energetic patterns within the body, and resisting or suppressing them can lead to inner conflict and suffering. Through practical techniques and insightful guidance, Dr. Hawkins provides readers with a road map to navigate their emotional landscapes and elevate their levels of consciousness. The Map of Consciousness®, a recurring theme in Hawkins's works, is employed to illustrate the vibrational frequencies of different emotional states, highlighting the transformative potential of letting go.

Letting Go encourages readers to foster forgiveness, acceptance, and love as essential components of the surrender process. Drawing on a blend of spiritual wisdom and psychological principles, the book resonates with those seeking to break free from the shackles of emotional burdens and step into a more liberated and authentic way of living. With practical exercises and profound insights, Dr. Hawkins guides readers toward the pathway of surrender, offering a compelling vision of the emotional and spiritual liberation that awaits those willing to let go.

Success Is for You: Using Heart-Centered Power Principles for Lasting Abundance and Fulfillment (2016)

A motivational guide that combines spiritual principles with practical strategies to help individuals achieve lasting success and fulfillment. The book revolves around the idea that true success is not only about external achievements but also about aligning one's life with heart-centered power principles.

Dr. Hawkins introduces the concept of heart-centered power, emphasizing qualities such as love, integrity, and compassion as essential elements in the pursuit of success. He suggests that success is not just a material or financial achievement but an alignment with higher states of consciousness and a life lived in harmony with universal principles.

The book offers practical insights and exercises to help readers overcome limiting beliefs, fears, and self-sabotaging patterns. Dr. Hawkins encourages a holistic approach to success, one that encompasses not only professional achievements but also personal growth, relationships, and spiritual well-being.

Success Is for You integrates Dr. Hawkins's spiritual teachings with actionable advice, making it a guide for individuals seeking a more profound and meaningful approach to success. By emphasizing heart-centered principles, the book aims to empower readers to create a life of abundance, authenticity, and lasting fulfillment.

Book of Slides: The Complete Collection Presented at the 2002–2011 Lectures with Clarifications (2018)

A comprehensive atlas of the vast terrain covered by Dr. Hawkins in his public monthly lectures during the years 2002 through 2011. It contains the compendium of his lecture slides, along with a summary of his teaching at each lecture. This book is filled with real-life examples, humorous anecdotes, and personal experiences of Doc never before found in written form.

Widely appreciated for his unusual capacity to illumine the Real in everyday terms, Dr. Hawkins lectured on such vital topics as the Nature of God, Nonduality, Self-Realization, Spirituality in the Modern World, Spiritual Community, Spiritual Teachers, the Way of Devotion, Qualities of the Spiritual Seeker, Love, Success, and Happiness.

The Map of Consciousness Explained: A Proven Energy Scale to Actualize Your Ultimate Potential (2020)

The Map of Consciousness Explained is an essential primer on Dr. Hawkins's teachings on human consciousness and their associated energy fields. Using muscle testing, Dr. Hawkins conducted more than 250,000 calibrations during 20 years of research to define a range of values, attitudes, and emotions that correspond to levels of consciousness. This range of values—along with a logarithmic scale of 1 to 1,000—became the Map of Consciousness®, which Dr. Hawkins first wrote about in *Power vs. Force*.

In this book, which is based on an audio program, readers will gain an introduction and deeper understanding of the Map, with visual charts and practical applications to help them heal, recover, and evolve to higher levels of consciousness and energy.

The Ego Is Not the Real You: Wisdom to Transcend the Mind and Realize the Self (2021)

A small collection of classic passages of wisdom. Learn to let go of the illusions of the ego and discover the real you with this collection of inspiring quotes on the ego, mind, and spiritual enlightenment from human-consciousness expert Dr. Hawkins.

Are you willing to let go of seeing yourself as the ego believes you to be? Are you willing to go further, to know that the ego itself is an illusion?

In this book, select teachings from Dr. Hawkins's extensive body of work will guide you in the process of realization, surrender, and transformation. When we let go of the old ways of thinking, our attachments, and the false promises of the ego, we discover the truth that we are one with All.

The Wisdom of Dr. David R. Hawkins: Classic Teachings on Spiritual Truth and Enlightenment (2022)

A compilation of the renowned spiritual teacher's timeless insights and teachings. Drawing from Dr. Hawkins's extensive body of work, the book offers a comprehensive overview of his philosophy and wisdom. Central to his teachings is the exploration of consciousness, the nature of reality, and the spiritual journey toward enlightenment.

The compilation covers a range of topics, including the power of love, the significance of surrender, and the transformative impact of raising one's level of consciousness.

This collection serves as a guide for those seeking spiritual truth and enlightenment, presenting Dr. Hawkins's teachings in a condensed and accessible format. It includes practical advice, anecdotes, and philosophical reflections aimed at inspiring individuals on their spiritual journeys. Overall, *The Wisdom of Dr. David R. Hawkins* is a valuable resource for those interested in delving into the profound teachings of this influential spiritual figure.

The Letting Go Guided Journal: How to Remove Your Inner Blocks to Happiness, Love, and Success (2022)

Based on Dr. Hawkins's classic work *Letting Go*, this guided mindfulness journal offers tools and techniques to help readers work through their feelings and truly let go of the inner blocks to peace that are holding them back. It is a perfect motivational gift for anyone seeking more balance, clarity, and positivity in their life, offering the reader a hands-on way to put the letting-go method into practice rather than just reading about it.

Readers work through exercises to help them to stop suppressing emotions, release resentments, overcome resistance, surrender the ego, deepen self-awareness, and more to find a path to inner freedom and find a newfound sense of self-assurance.

In the World but Not of It: Transforming Everyday Experience into a Spiritual Path (2023)

Based on the audio program of the same name, this book shares Dr. Hawkins's timeless insights on why certain spiritual experiences only provide temporary enlightenment. In the process, he explains how to turn normal activities into your spiritual practice.

Capturing Dr. Hawkins's signature startling humor, captivating brilliance, and deep understanding of the path of humanity and higher consciousness, readers learn about various topics, including raising the consciousness of the world, being accountable to their decisions, what to embrace and what to avoid in our technologically driven world, and how to avoid stress.

The Highest Level of Enlightenment: Transcend the Levels of Consciousness for Total Self-Realization (2024)

In this profound book, based on a popular audio program, Dr. David Hawkins gives a primer on his world-famous Map of Consciousness® that will help the reader embark on their own journey to an advanced state of consciousness.

Dr. Hawkins's research is based on a well-established science called kinesiology, which has to do with the testing of an all-or-none muscle response stimulus. A positive stimulus generates a strong muscle response, and a negative stimulus results in a demonstrable weakening of the test muscle. Clinical kinesiological muscle testing as a diagnostic technique has been verified widely over the past 25 years.

David Hawkins, M.D., Ph.D, conducted a 29-year study that demonstrated that the human body becomes stronger or weaker depending on a person's mental state. He created a scale from 1 to 1,000 that mapped human consciousness. Furthermore, he demonstrated that this map can be used as a blueprint to reach higher states of consciousness that can be identified simply by applying a small amount of pressure on an outstretched arm!

Not only that, but this simple method has also been demonstrated to be an effective tool for instantly calibrating human consciousness. Dr. Hawkins created a scale of consciousness based on current discoveries in advanced theoretical physics and the nonlinear dynamics of chaos theory. And this Map of Consciousness® now makes it possible for anyone to advance toward higher levels of enlightenment faster than ever imagined!

The Path to Spiritual Advancement: How to Transcend the Ego and Experience the Presence of God (2024)

The first volume of a new six-book series, this book comprises the transcribed lectures presented by Dr. Hawkins in January and February of 2002. This book is as pure and as close to Dr. Hawkins's voice as possible, though redundancies and grammatical inconsistencies have been deleted.

The teachings included discuss the purpose of Dr. Hawkins's work, the Map of Consciousness® and how it came to be, the illusion of causality as the great block to spiritual advancement, the role of karma in a person's life, existence versus non-existence, and many other topics.

Dr. Hawkins tells us that we are safe and to trust that safety in the Truth and Loving Presence of Divinity itself. We hope this volume will give you a sense of that love and safety and spur you onward and upward.

Veritas Publishing Streaming Video Service

All of Dr. Hawkins's lectures are available through **veritaspub.com/streaming-product-information**. An MP3 format for all lectures is available through Audible.

NOTES

Introduction

1. *Power vs. Force*, lii.
2. *Letting Go*, 46.

Chapter 1

1. April 2002 lecture.
2. *Discovery of the Presence of God*, 20.
3. September 2002 lecture.
4. September 2002 lecture.
5. June 2002 lecture.
6. *Healing and Recovery*, 456.
7. *Discovery of the Presence of God*, 20.
8. *The Eye of the I*, 164.
9. March 2002 lecture.
10. *Healing and Recovery*, 457.
11. February 2002 lecture.
12. *Discovery of the Presence of God*, 21.
13. February 2002 lecture.
14. *Discovery of the Presence of God*, 21.
15. February 2002 lecture.
16. March 2002 lecture.

Chapter 2

1. *I*, xxiv.
2. August 2009 lecture.
3. September 2002 lecture.
4. September 2002 lecture.

Chapter 3

1. *The Eye of the I*, 383.
2. *Power vs. Force*, xlix.
3. *Power vs. Force*, l.
4. *Letting Go*, 88.
5. *Letting Go*, 89.
6. *Letting Go*, 87.
7. May 2002 lecture.
8. *Healing and Recovery*, 271.

Chapter 4

1. *Healing and Recovery*, 43.
2. "Schizophrenia: An Evolutionary Defense Against Severe Stress," 210.
3. "Revisiting the Use of the Hoffer Osmond Diagnostic Test in Mental Health."
4. *The Vitamin B-3 Therapy*, 18.

Chapter 5

1. *Power vs. Force*, 205.
2. *Healing and Recovery*, 396.
3. *Power vs. Force*, 206–7.
4. *Power vs. Force*, 207.
5. "What Does 'Surrender' Mean?"
6. *Power vs. Force*, 204.
7. "What We Believe."
8. *Discovery of the Presence of God*, 21.
9. *Discovery of the Presence of God*, 21.
10. *Healing and Recovery*, 459.
11. *Discovery of the Presence of God*, 21–22.
12. *Discovery of the Presence of God*, 22.
13. *The Eye of the I*, 23.
14. *The Vitamin B-3 Therapy*, 23.
15. "Community Involvement in Orthomolecular Therapy," 205.

Chapter 6

1. *Power vs. Force*, 382–83.
2. April 2002 lecture.

3. Laughlin, "Consciousness, Medicine, & Healing."
4. Colin, "Meet the Psychedelic Boom's First Responders."
5. Gee, "As Psychedelics Return."
6. Laughlin, "Consciousness, Medicine, & Healing."
7. *Dialogues*, 30.
8. *Healing and Recovery*, 299.
9. *Healing and Recovery*, 465.
10. *Letting Go*, 249.

Chapter 7

1. January 2002 lecture.
2. March 2002 lecture.
3. Black, *Love Me? Love Yourself*, 6.
4. Black, *Love Me? Love Yourself*, 7.
5. The Sedona Method, "Lester Created the Sedona Method to Save His Own Life."
6. "The Scale of Action in Emotions."
7. "The 9 Fundamental Emotional States from the Sedona Method."
8. "Sedona Releasing Method," chapter 20, 10.
9. *Letting Go*, xxii.
10. *Letting Go*, xxi–xxii.
11. "Dr. David Hawkins Praises Sedona Method."
12. *Power vs. Force*, xv.
13. February 2002 lecture.
14. March 2002 lecture.
15. *Transcending the Levels of Consciousness*, 408.
16. Laughlin, "Consciousness, Medicine, & Healing."
17. *Power vs. Force*, 76–77.
18. ACIM, "An Introduction to *A Course In Miracles*."
19. Laughlin, "Consciousness, Medicine, & Healing."
20. February 2002 lecture.
21. *Healing and Recovery*, 458.
22. April 2002 lecture.

Chapter 8

1. *Transcending the Levels of Consciousness*, 405.
2. *Transcending the Levels of Consciousness*, 408.
3. *Discovery of the Presence of God*, 36.
4. *The Map of Consciousness Explained*, 261.

Chapter 9

1. January 2002 lecture.
2. *Healing and Recovery*, 469.
3. *Healing and Recovery*, 470.
4. *Transcending the Levels of Consciousness*, 404.
5. *Discovery of the Presence of God*, 135–36.
6. *Transcending the Levels of Consciousness*, 101.
7. *I*, 384.
8. *Transcending the Levels of Consciousness*, 102.
9. *Discovery of the Presence of God*, 137.
10. *Transcending the Levels of Consciousness*, 302.
11. *Discovery of the Presence of God*, 138.
12. *Life with "Doc,"* 75.
13. *Life with "Doc,"* 15.
14. *Life with "Doc,"* 17.
15. *Truth vs. Falsehood*, 451.
16. *Power vs. Force*, xlix–l.
17. "A Map of Consciousness" lecture.
18. *The Map of Consciousness Explained*, 50.
19. *The Map of Consciousness Explained*, 55.
20. *The Map of Consciousness Explained*, 25.
21. *The Map of Consciousness Explained*, xiv, xv.
22. "A Map of Consciousness" lecture.
23. *Truth vs. Falsehood*, 451.
24. *Truth vs. Falsehood*, 452.

Chapter 10

1. *I*, 355.
2. *I*, 356.
3. *I*, 357.
4. *Life with "Doc,"* 58.
5. *I*, 356.
6. December 2006 lecture.
7. *Life with "Doc,"* 26.
8. *Power vs. Force*, 73.
9. *Power vs. Force*, 94.

Notes

Chapter 11

1. *Life with "Doc,"* 31.
2. *Life with "Doc,"* 109.
3. April 2002 lecture.
4. *Truth vs. Falsehood*, 34.
5. *Truth vs. Falsehood*, ix.
6. *Life with "Doc,"* 79.
7. *Life with "Doc,"* 81.
8. March 2008 lecture.
9. *Truth vs. Falsehood*, 36.
10. *Transcending the Levels of Consciousness*, xiii
11. *Discovery of the Presence of God*, ix.
12. *Life with "Doc,"* 150.
13. *Reality, Spirituality, and Modern Man*, xiv.
14. *Reality, Spirituality, and Modern Man*, xxix.
15. *Healing and Recovery*, xiv.

Chapter 12

1. September 2011 lecture.
2. September 2011 lecture.
3. *Healing and Recovery*, 470–71.
4. *Life with "Doc,"* 144.
5. *Life with "Doc,"* 151.
6. *Healing and Recovery*, 472.
7. September 2011 lecture.

REFERENCES

BOOKS BY DR. HAWKINS

Hawkins, David R. *Dialogues on Consciousness and Spirituality.* Sedona, AZ: Veritas Publishing, 1997.

Hawkins, David R. *Discovery of the Presence of God: Devotional Nonduality.* Sedona, AZ: Veritas Publishing, 2006.

Hawkins, David R. *The Eye of the I: From Which Nothing Is Hidden.* Sedona, AZ: Veritas Publishing, 2001.

Hawkins, David R. *Healing and Recovery.* Sedona, AZ: Veritas Publishing, 2009.

Hawkins, David R. *I: Reality and Subjectivity.* Sedona, AZ: Veritas Publishing, 2003.

Hawkins, David R. *Letting Go: The Pathway of Surrender.* Sedona, AZ: Veritas Publishing, 2012.

Hawkins, David R. *The Map of Consciousness Explained: A Proven Energy Scale to Actualize Your Ultimate Potential.* Sedona, AZ: Veritas Publishing, 2020.

Hawkins, David R. *Power vs. Force: The Hidden Determinants of Human Behavior.* Sedona, AZ: Veritas Publishing, 1994.

Hawkins, David R. *Reality, Spirituality, and Modern Man.* Sedona, AZ: Veritas Publishing, 2008.

Hawkins, David R. *Transcending the Levels of Consciousness: The Stairway to Enlightenment.* Sedona, AZ: Veritas Publishing, 2006.

Hawkins, David R. *Truth vs. Falsehood: How to Tell the Difference.* Sedona, AZ: Veritas Publishing, 2005.

LECTURES BY DR. HAWKINS

Hawkins, David R. "A Map of Consciousness." Lecture from the archival Office Visits lecture series. Courtesy of Veritas Publishing.

Hawkins, David R. "Advaita: The Way to God Through Mind." August 2002 lecture from The Way to God lecture series. Courtesy of Veritas Publishing.

Hawkins, David R. "Causality: The Ego's Foundation." January 2002 lecture from The Way to God lecture series. Courtesy of Veritas Publishing.

Hawkins, David R. "The Clear Pathway to Enlightenment." March 2008 lecture from the Advanced Spiritual Awareness lecture series. Courtesy of Veritas Publishing.

Hawkins, David R. "Devotion: The Way to God Through the Heart." September 2002 lecture from The Way to God lecture series. Courtesy of Veritas Publishing.

Hawkins, David R. "Emotions and Sensations." April 2004 lecture from the Transcending the Mind lecture series. Courtesy of Veritas Publishing.

Hawkins, David R. "The Levels of Consciousness: Subjective & Social Consequences." March 2002 lecture from The Way to God lecture series. Courtesy of Veritas Publishing.

Hawkins, David R. "Love." September 2011 lecture. Courtesy of Veritas Publishing.

Hawkins, David R. "Is the Miraculous Real?" December 2006 lecture from Transcending Levels of Consciousness lecture series. Courtesy of Veritas Publishing.

Hawkins, David R. "Perception and Illusion: Distortions of Reality." May 2002 lecture from The Way to God lecture series. Courtesy of Veritas Publishing.

Hawkins, David R. "Positionality and Duality: Transcending the Opposites." April 2002 lecture from The Way to God lecture series. Courtesy of Veritas Publishing.

Hawkins, David R. "Radical Subjectivity: The 'I' of Self." February 2002 lecture from The Way to God lecture series. Courtesy of Veritas Publishing.

Hawkins, David R. "Realizing the Root of Consciousness: Meditative and Contemplative Techniques." June 2002 lecture from The Way to God lecture series. Courtesy of Veritas Publishing.

References

OTHER WRITINGS BY DR. HAWKINS

Hawkins, David R. "Community Involvement in Orthomolecular Therapy." *Orthomolecular Psychiatry* 6(2): 203–11. 1977. isom.ca/wp-content/uploads/2020/01/JOM_1977_06_2_09_Community_Involvement_in_Orthomolecular_Therapy.pdf.

Hawkins, David R. "Sedona Releasing Method." Printed manuscript from Veritas Publishing, 1984.

Hawkins, David R., Aaron M. Bortin, and Richard P. Runyon. "Orthomolecular Psychiatry: Niacin and Megavitamin Therapy." *Psychosomatics* 1970 Sep–Oct;11(5):517–21. doi: 10.1016/S0033-3182(70)71622-8.

OTHER SOURCES

902d Military Intelligence Group. "Gondola Wish Assessment Report (U)." Central Intelligence Agency. August 25, 1978. Declassified December 31, 2008. cia.gov/readingroom/document/cia-rdp96-00788r002000160001-3.

Alcoholics Anonymous. "The Start and Growth of A.A." Accessed March 28, 2024. aa.org/the-start-and-growth-of-aa.

Arizona Commerce. "Appendix A to Report No. 13, 'Local Population Estimates of Arizona' as of July 1, 1981." Accessed March 28, 2024. azcommerce.com/media/cw5nzrto/population-counts-of-az-1980-and-1970.pdf.

Attitudinal Healing International. "What Is Attitudinal Healing?" Accessed March 28, 2024. ahinternational.org/about/what-is-attitudinal-healing.

Ayres, Toraya. "The History of New Age Sedona." Originally published as a book by High Mountain Training and Publishing Company, Cedar City, Utah. 1997. lovesedona.com/history1.htm.

Bargh, John and Ezequiel Morsella. "The Unconscious Mind." *Perspectives in Psychological Science* 3:1, 73–79. January 2008. ncbi.nlm.nih.gov/pmc/articles/PMC2440575.

Bartley, William Warren, III. *Werner Erhard: The Transformation of a Man, The Founding of est.* Clarkson Potter, 1988.

Better Life Coaches. "Hale Dwoskin: Letting Go!" YouTube. February 20, 2002. youtube.com/watch?v=L-h7EwvuKdo&ab_channel=BetterLife Coaches.

Black, Vern. *Love Me? Love Yourself.* San Francisco, CA: Vern Black and Associates. 1983.

Carter, Stephen. "Orthomolecular Medicine." *Integral Medicine* 18:3, 74. June 2019. ncbi.nlm.nih.gov/pmc/articles/PMC7217400.

Centers for Spiritual Living. "What We Believe." Accessed March 28, 2024. omcsl.org/copy-of-what-we-believe.

Colin, Chris. "Meet the Psychedelic Boom's First Responders." *Wired.* June 29, 2023. wired.com/story/meet-the-psychedelic-booms-first-responders.

Gee, Dana. "As Psychedelics Return So Does the Story of New Westminster's Hollywood Hospital." *Vancouver Sun.* July 6, 2022. vancouversun.com/entertainment/books/the-acid-room-reflects-back-on-groundbreaking-and-mind-blowing-hollywood-hospital.

Gioia, Joe. "The American Way of Zen: How It Arrived and Why It Thrived." Magellan TV. August 7, 2022. magellantv.com/articles/the-american-way-of-zen-how-it-arrived-and-why-it-thrived.

Greenblatt, James. "Alcoholism, Vitamin B3 & the Future of Psychiatry." Psychiatry Redefined. January 5, 2023. psychiatryredefined.org/alcoholism-treatment-vitamin-b3.

Hawkins, Susan. *Life with "Doc": My Husband and My Teacher, Dr. David R. Hawkins.* Sedona, AZ: Veritas Publishing, 2022.

Hoffer, A. "Schizophrenia: An Evolutionary Defense Against Severe Stress." *Journal of Orthomolecular Medicine* 9(4). 1994. isom.ca/wp-content/uploads/2020/01/JOM_1994_09_4_03_Schizophrenia_An_Evolutionary_Defence_Against_Severe-.pdf.

The Institute of Chiropractic & Acupuncture Therapy. "Muscle Testing 101: How it Works! / SuperDocDC.com / 801-567-0557." YouTube. September 20, 2016. youtube.com/watch?v=UCYK8EcxAcw&ab_channel=TheInstituteofChiropractic%26AcupunctureTherapy.

Josefson, Deborah. "Rebirthing Therapy Banned After Girl Died in 70 Minute Struggle" *British Medical Journal.* 322(7293): 1014. April 28, 2001. ncbi.nlm.nih.gov/pmc/articles/PMC1174742.

Kendler, Kenneth S., Katheryn Tabb, and John Wright. "The Emergence of Psychiatry: 1650–1850." *American Journal of Psychiatry* 179(5). March 25, 2022. doi.org/10.1176/appi.ajp.21060614.

Laughlin, Matt. "Consciousness, Medicine, & Healing: An Interview with David R. Hawkins, M.D., Ph.D.—Part I." Nightingale-Conant. 2012. nightingale.com/newsletters/537a.

References

Lea, A. J. "Adrenochrome as the Cause of Schizophrenia: Investigation of Some Deductions from This Hypothesis." *Journal of Mental Science* 101(424): 538–47. 1955. Published online by Cambridge University Press. February 8, 2018. doi:10.1192/bjp.101.424.538. cambridge.org/core/journals/journal-of-mental-science/article/abs/adrenochrome-as-the-cause-of-schizophrenia-investigation-of-some-deduction from-this-hypothesis/8CD098ECD668B1E3636589C13AEA0214.

Milwaukee Public Library. "David G. Hooker." Accessed March 28, 2024. content.mpl.org/digital/collection/MilwMayors/id/18.

National Institute on Alcohol Abuse and Alcoholism. "Alcohol's Effects on Health." 2021. niaaa.nih.gov/publications/cycle-alcohol-addiction.

Naval History and Heritage Command. "Typhoons and Hurricanes: Pacific Typhoon at Okinawa, October 1945." November 13, 2017. history.navy.mil/research/library/online-reading-room/title-list-alphabetically/p/pacific-typhoon-october-1945.html.

Nichols, David. E. "Psychedelics." *Pharmacological Reviews* 68(2): 264–355. April 2016. doi.org/10.1124/pr.115.011478.

Pauling, Linus. "Orthomolecular Psychiatry: Varying the Concentrations of Substances Normally Present in the Human Body May Control Mental Disease." *Science* 160(3825): 265–71. April 19, 1968. doi.org/10.1126/science.160.3825.265.

QAHomeStudy. "Dr. George Goodheart Discusses the Origins of Applied Kinesiology." YouTube. January 22, 2019. youtube.com/watch?v=gYCz5-UvD0&ab_channel=QAHomeStudy.

Saxon, Wolfgang. "Lionel Ovesey, Psychoanalyst, Is Dead at 80." *New York Times.* May 23, 1995. nytimes.com/1995/05/23/obituaries/lionel-ovesey-psychoanalyst-is-dead-at-80.html.

"The Scale of Action in Emotions." Mind Freedom handout, 1974. Provided by Susan Hawkins.

"Dr. David Hawkins Praises Sedona Method." *The Sedona Magazine*, September 1979. Provided by Susan Hawkins.

The Sedona Method. "Lester Created the Sedona Method to Save His Own Life." Accessed March 28, 2024. sedona.com/Lester-Levenson.

The Sedona Method. "The Sedona Method: What Is It." YouTube. September 16, 2020. youtube.com/watch?v=zdAi_snJKBI&t=11s&ab_channel=TheSedonaMethod.

The Sedona Method. "What Is the Sedona Method." Accessed March 28,

2024. sedona.com/What-Is-The-Sedona-Method.

Self Help for Life. "The 9 Fundamental Emotional States from the Sedona Method." YouTube. March 19, 2018. youtube.com/watch?v=cjWaM VwAPMs&ab_channel=SelfHelpforLife.

Skutch, Robert. "The Incredible Untold Story Behind . . . A Course in Miracles (Part I)." *New Realities Magazine*. July-August 1984. acim.org /archives/articles/incredible-untold-story-behind-acim-part-i.

Stark, Paul, Jean Kemble, and Iris Levy. "Basic Freudian Concepts." Empire State College. June 2006. empire2.esc.edu/FACULTYWEB /JANETBACHANT.NSF/003a7ad981f4fb2085256889006cd 9b4/7d3af28382433ae2852571d9006dd2df?OpenDocument.

Tiebout, Harry. "The Ego Factors in Surrender in Alcoholism." Accessed March 28, 2024. silkworth.net/alcoholics-anonymous/the-ego-factors in-surrender-in-alcoholism.

Tiebout, Harry. "What Does 'Surrender' Mean?" *Grapevine*, April 1963 .Published on Get Up, Get Sober, Get Out. August 10, 2020. gugogs. org/2020/08/10/what-does-surrender-mean-grapevine-april-1963-dr harry-tiebout.

Uboat.net. "Allied Warships: USS YMS-46 (YMS-46)." Accessed March 28, 2024. uboat.net/allies/warships/ship/9466.html.

Werner Erhard and est. "Werner Erhard." YouTube. August 22, 2008. youtube.com/watch?v=mMeXmFVq6cY&t=67s&ab_channel=werner erhardandest.

Wick, Jeannette. "The History of Benzodiazepines." *The Consultant Pharmacist*. September 2013. 9, 538–48. doi.org/10.4140/tcp.n.2013.538.

World Health Organization. "History of the Polio Vaccine." January 31, 2018. who.int/news-room/spotlight/history-of-vaccination/history of-polio-vaccination.

Wilson, Bill. *The Vitamin B-3 Therapy: A Second Communication to A.A.'s Physicians*. February 1968. aaagnostica.org/wp-content/uploads/2016/05/ The-Vitamin-B-3-Therapy.pdf.

ABOUT THE AUTHOR

Susan Hawkins serves as president of the Institute for Spiritual Research Inc., the foundation started by her husband, Dr. David R. Hawkins (d. 2012). He said she was the "fulcrum" that made possible the sharing of his knowledge and presence in the world. He pointed to her keen intuition, personal warmth, and crucial companionship. She always traveled with him during his years of public teaching, and he was never onstage without her. She joined him in several video-recorded dialogues on practical topics such as "Improving Your Relationships" and "Live Your Life Like a Prayer." After his passing in 2012, she continued to hold a yearly gathering in Sedona, Arizona, until 2019, when she began offering regular virtual gatherings for inspiration and fellowship. For more information, go to the Veritas Publishing website: **www.veritaspub.com**.

ABOUT DR. DAVID R. HAWKINS

Dr. David R. Hawkins (1927–2012) was renowned as a physician, author, lecturer, and researcher of consciousness. After serving in the United States Navy during World War II, he graduated from the Medical College of Wisconsin in 1953. For the next 25 years, he lived in New York, where his pioneering work as a psychiatrist brought major clinical breakthroughs, especially in the treatment of schizophrenia and alcoholism. His research findings were published widely in medical, scientific, and psychoanalytic journals. As medical director of the North Nassau Mental Health Center (1956–1980) and director of research at Brunswick Hospital (1968–1979) on Long Island, he had the largest practice in New York.

In 1973, Dr. Hawkins co-authored *Orthomolecular Psychiatry* with Nobel laureate chemist Linus Pauling, initiating a new field within psychiatry and leading to appearances on numerous talk shows. He spoke at the Oxford Forum and Westminster Abbey, as well as Harvard University, University of Argentina, University of Notre Dame, University of California, Fordham University, and the Institute for Noetic Sciences. He also served as a psychiatric advisor to Catholic, Protestant, and Buddhist monasteries.

Dr. Hawkins received numerous recognitions for his scientific and humanitarian contributions, including: the Huxley Award for the "Inestimable Contribution to the Alleviation of Human Suffering"; Physician's Recognition Award by the American Medical Association; 50-Year Distinguished Life Fellow by the American Psychiatric Association; the Orthomolecular Medicine Hall of Fame; Who's Who in the World; and a nomination for the prestigious Templeton Prize, which honors progress in science and religion.

In 1983, Dr. Hawkins established the Institute for Spiritual Research Inc., a nonprofit organization dedicated to consciousness research. During the 1980s, his lectures at such events as the First National Conference on Addictions and Consciousness (1985) and Whole Life Expo (1986), both held in California, recontextualized addiction by illuminating the underlying spiritual drive for inner peace and how to cultivate it apart from substances. During the 1990s, he served as the chief of staff at Mingus Mountain Estate Residential Treatment Center for adolescent girls in Prescott Valley and was the consulting psychiatrist for several recovery houses in Arizona.

Dr. Hawkins spent the last three decades of his life in Arizona, working to correlate the seemingly disparate domains of science and spirituality. In 1995, at the age of 68, he received a Ph.D. in health and human services. That same year saw the publication of his book *Power vs. Force*, which was ultimately translated into 25 languages with over a million copies sold, and evoking praise from such notables as Mother Teresa and Sam Walton. *Power vs. Force* presented his trademarked Map of Consciousness®, now used by health professionals, university professors, government officials, and business executives worldwide. Many other books followed.

About Dr. David R. Hawkins

In recognition of Dr. Hawkins's contributions to humanity, he was knighted in 1996 by the Sovereign Order of the Hospitaliers of St. John of Jerusalem by authority of the Priory of King Valdemar the Great. From 1998 to 2011, Dr. Hawkins traveled widely as a lecturer throughout the United States and overseas, speaking to sold-out audiences about the science of consciousness and the reality of advanced spiritual states. In 2000, he was bestowed the title "Tae Ryoung Sun Kak Tosa" (Teacher of Enlightenment) in Seoul, South Korea. His final lecture, entitled "Love," occurred in September 2011 and was attended by 1,700 people from around the world. Dr. Hawkins was active to the very end. Just before his passing in September 2012, he completed a video-recorded dialogue series and finished his twelfth book.

Throughout Dr. Hawkins's life, he participated in a wide range of civic and professional endeavors, often in leadership roles. As a physician, he co-founded or served as medical advisor for many organizations, including the Schizophrenia Foundations of New York and Long Island, the Attitudinal Healing Center of Long Island, the New York Association of Holistic Health Centers, and the Academy of Orthomolecular Psychiatry. He was co-director of the Masters Gallery of Fine Arts.

Born with an exceptionally high IQ, he became a member of Mensa International in 1963. As a young doctor, he was attracted to Buddhism and joined the first Zen Institute in the United States. At the time of his death, he had been a member of St. Andrew's Episcopal Church for many years. He was the first president of the Country and Western Dance Club of Sedona and a member of the Veterans of Foreign Wars, American Legion, and Sedona Elks Lodge. He was an archer, carpenter, blacksmith, musician (bagpiper, violinist, pianist), designer of prize-winning 16th-century French Norman architecture, and lover of animals.

Internationally, Dr. Hawkins was the founder of Devotional Nonduality (2003), a spiritual pathway that applies the core truths of the world's great traditions: kindness and compassion for all of life (including oneself), unconditional love, humility, inquiry into the nature of existence, surrender, and self-realization. Since 2002, "Hawkins Study Groups" have autonomously sprung up in many cities around the world, from Los Angeles to Seoul, from Cape Town to Melbourne; the groups study and practice the principles of his books, such as: "We change the world not by what we say or do but as a consequence of what we have become." His life exemplified that principle.

We hope you enjoyed this Hay House book. If you'd like to receive our online catalogue featuring additional information on Hay House books and products, please contact:

Hay House UK Ltd
1st Floor, Crawford Corner,
91–93 Baker Street, London W1U 6QQ
Tel: +44 (0)20 3927 7290; www.hayhouse.co.uk

Published in the United States of America by:
Hay House LLC
PO Box 5100, Carlsbad, CA 92018-5100
Tel: (760) 431-7695 or (800) 654-5126
www.hayhouse.com

Published in Australia by:
Hay House Australia Publishing Pty Ltd
18/36 Ralph St., Alexandria NSW 2015
Tel: +61 (02) 9669 4299
www.hayhouse.com.au

Published in India by:
Hay House Publishers (India) Pvt Ltd
Muskaan Complex, Plot No. 3,
B-2, Vasant Kunj, New Delhi 110 070
Tel: +91 11 41761620
www.hayhouse.co.in

Let Your Soul Grow

Experience life-changing transformation – one video at a time – with guidance from the world's leading experts.

www.healyourlifeplus.com

HAY HOUSE
Online Video Courses

Your journey to a better life starts with figuring out which path is best for you. Hay House Online Courses provide guidance in mental and physical health, personal finance, telling your unique story, and so much more!

LEARN HOW TO:

- choose your words and actions wisely so you can tap into life's magic
- clear the energy in yourself and your environments for improved clarity, peace, and joy
- forgive, visualize, and trust in order to create a life of authenticity and abundance
- manifest lifelong health by improving nutrition, reducing stress, improving sleep, and more
- create your own unique angelic communication toolkit to help you to receive clear messages for yourself and others
- use the creative power of the quantum realm to create health and well-being

To find the guide for your journey, visit www.HayHouseU.com.

HAY HOUSE
online learning

CONNECT WITH
HAY HOUSE
ONLINE

🌐 hayhouse.co.uk   **f** @hayhouse

📷 @hayhouseuk   🦋 @hayhouseuk.bsky.social

♪ @hayhouseuk   ▶ @HayHousePresents

Find out all about our latest books & card decks • Be the first to know about exclusive discounts • Interact with our authors in live broadcasts • Celebrate the cycle of the seasons with us • Watch free videos from your favourite authors • Connect with like-minded souls

'The gateways to wisdom and knowledge
are always open.'

Louise Hay